FRENCH-CANADIAN &
QUÉBÉCOIS NOVELS

Perspectives on Canadian Culture

JUDITH SALTMAN
Modern Canadian Children's Books

EUGENE BENSON & L.W. CONNOLLY
English-Canadian Theatre

DAVID CLANDFIELD
Canadian Film

MICHELLE GADPAILLE
The Canadian Short Story

EDITH FOWKE
Canadian Folklore

DOUGLAS FETHERLING
The Rise of the Canadian Newspaper

BEN-Z. SHEK
French-Canadian & Québécois Novels

FRENCH-CANADIAN & QUÉBÉCOIS NOVELS

Ben-Z. Shek

Toronto   OXFORD UNIVERSITY PRESS   1991

Oxford University Press, 70 Wynford Drive, Don Mills, Ontario M3C 1J9

Toronto Oxford New York
Delhi Bombay Calcutta Madras Karachi Petaling Jaya
Singapore Hong Kong Tokyo Nairobi Dar es Salaam
Cape Town Melbourne Auckland

and associated companies in
Berlin Ibadan

P.B/34

For
JEAN, ELLIOT, GHITTA

The wood-cut on the front cover is by
Jean Lébédeff and is among the illustrations in
an edition of Louis Hémon's *Maria Chapdelaine*
published in Paris in 1936.

Canadian Cataloguing in Publication Data

Shek, Ben-Zion, 1927
French-Canadian and Québécois novels
(Perspectives on Canadian culture)
Includes bibliographical references and index.
ISBN 0-19-540723-7

1. Canadian fiction(French) - History and criticism.*
2. Canadian fiction (French) - Translations into English -
History and criticism.* 3. English fiction - Translations
from French - History and criticism. 4. Quebec
(Province) in literature. I. Title. II. Series.

PS8187.S45 1991 C843.009 C91-093779-6 PQ3912.S45 1991

CONTENTS

PREFACE

The aim of this book is to give an overview of the novel's evolution and modern flowering in francophone Quebec literature, from the beginnings in 1837 until the end of the 1980s. The term 'French-Canadian' in the title refers to works written before the Quiet Revolution of the 1960s, but also includes writings by non-French-Canadians like Louis Hémon.[*] I have included for obvious reasons the works of Gabrielle Roy and Antonine Maillet, though they were not born in Quebec. Their careers, however, were greatly encouraged by the growing strength of the Québécois literary network—and they settled in Quebec.

The format of the *Perspectives on Canadian Culture* series imposed certain constraints. Because of limitations of space the concentration is on major (or historically significant) writers, and for very prolific writers I have been obliged to discuss only a selection of their novels. Furthermore, I have been asked to devote my discussions mainly to works that have been published in English translation. The English title is noted only once; an asterisk indicates a translation with the same title as the French original. (Translators' names are given in Appendix II.) On the subject of translation, all translated quotations from both previously translated and untranslated texts are my own.

The book is divided into five chapters, plus a short Conclusion, and an Appendix on translation. Chapter 1 covers the first century of development, from *L'Influence d'un livre* (1837) by Philippe Aubert de Gaspé *fils*, to Félix-Antoine Savard's *Menaud, Maître*

---

[*] 'French-Canadian' here does not, unfortunately, include francophone authors who live(d) outside Quebec. They should be treated in a separate study because of the unique socio-cultural context in which they write.

draveur (1937). Chapter 2 treats especially the emergence of urban social realism (Gabrielle Roy and Roger Lemelin), and its roots in Ringuet's *Trente arpents* and Germaine Guèvremont's *Le Survenant*, as well as the early works of two of Quebec's best-known writers, Yves Thériault and André Langevin. Chapter 3 covers the period of the Quiet Revolution; Chapter 4 the development of feminist writing; and Chapter 5 the writings of the seventies and eighties.

Every literary critic brings his or her own biases into play. My teaching and critical writing over a quarter of a century have concentrated on a socio-critical and ideological reading of French-Canadian and Québécois texts, and much of what I have to say is coloured by these approaches. I have kept in mind, however, other more exclusively text-oriented critical methods that have come to the fore during the same period, and hope that their insights will also be reflected in these pages.

I wish to thank warmly several people whose help has been most appreciated: my indefatigable editor, William Toye, who also conceived the idea for this book; several colleagues who read selected chapters — David M. Hayne, Jacques Allard, Barbara Godard, Patricia Smart; and my son Elliot, who helped me with the Appendixes on translation and translated novels. The responsibility for the content, however, rests entirely with me.

1

THE LONG GESTATION:
1837-1937

It is well known that mercantilist France did not permit the setting up of printing presses in its colony, New France, insisting that all publications of whatever kind be published in Paris. Nevertheless much writing in a variety of genres was inspired by contacts with Canada and its aboriginal inhabitants, and some of these were printed soon after completion, while others had to wait for years or even decades. Among the writings of New France were accounts of their voyages by Jacques Cartier and Samuel de Champlain, those of explorers Jolliet and d'Iberville, the annual Jesuit missionaries' reports to their superiors in the mother country issued under the name *Relations* (1632-1672), detailed ethnographic descriptions of Amerindian life by Sagard and more fanciful ones by LaHontan, the massive correspondence of Marie de l'Incarnation and that of Élisabeth Bégon, the annals of the Hôtel-Dieu de Montréal by Marie Morin, Pierre Boucher's inventory of the colony's resources, and historical accounts by Lescarbot, Dollier de Casson, and Charlevoix. Cartier's texts are believed to have influenced the subsequent literary production of Rabelais and Montaigne.

No novels emerged during the French regime. This genre had its beginnings in France as early as the sixteenth century, yet it would be some three hundred years before it made its appearance in French Canada. As for *reading* fiction, the Catholic clergy, whose power actually increased following the British Conquest,* lost no

---

*From the beginning of British rule, the francophones already began to differentiate themselves from the new rulers by referring to that event as *la Cession* (the ceding, or surrender).

time in denouncing such 'dangerous' books. As early as 1771, for example, Mgr Briand, Bishop of Quebec, urged his parishioners to 'stop reading those impious works that are spreading through the diocese.' In the 1840s, Bishop Bourget of Montreal led a campaign against 'the reading of immoral novels', and in Chauveau's *Charles Guérin* (1853) there is a reference to an *auto-da-fé* that nearly destroyed the entire library of M. Guérin senior, and may have been based on fact. In the postscript to another novel, published in serial form in 1846, Patrice Lacombe's *La Terre paternelle*, we read: 'Let's leave their blood-soaked novels to the old countries spoiled by civilization, and paint the child of the land the way he really is . . .' When Quebec novelists did begin to publish in the nineteenth century, they would write a preface denouncing their very genre, or disclaim their work's fictional nature. Antoine Gérin-Lajoie writes about his *Jean Rivard* (1862, 1864): 'This is not a novel . . .', and a critic claimed that this influential work was a 'faithful sketch of . . . a young Canadian pioneer . . .' Jules-Paul Tardivel, in his futuristic *Pour la patrie* (1895)/*For My Country*, prefaced the book by noting that 'the modern novel, and especially the French novel . . . seems to be an arm forged by Satan to destroy the human race.' Réjean Beaudoin has said that the call in 1861 by the leading literary ideologue, abbé Henri-Raymond Casgrain, for writers to draw on legends as major sources for literary creativity was a tactic for turning authors away from writing novels: 'One of the essential functions of the legend seems to have been to build a dike against the popularity of the modern novel . . . French-Canadian writers were urged to emulate the simplicity and purity of folk imagery, that direct reflection of the beauty of traditional folkways.' In 1866 Casgrain traced the main lines of a national and religious literature, which, he said, would be 'chaste and pure like the virginal mantle of our long winters . . . It will have none of the masks of modern realism, that manifestation of impious and materialist thought.'

These factors explain the slow emergence of the novel form in Quebec, as well as the fact that the first novelist, the twenty-three-year-old **Philippe Aubert de Gaspé** *fils* (1814-41), and his more famous father—who, it is believed, authored parts of his son's novel, *L'Influence d'un livre* (1837), as well as his own classic, *Les Anciens Canadiens* (1863)—both made ample use of legends in these two works. In fact, in both the central plot is interrupted by the insertion of legends and songs drawn from folk traditions. André Senécal has rightly stressed that from a generic point of view *L'Influence d'un livre* is nothing more than the outline of a novel.

Three narrative elements intertwine in this primitive text: the story of the search of an impoverished alchemist, Charles Amand, for the philosopher's stone that will make him rich, inspired by the manual of Albert le Petit; the murder of the peddler Guillemette by the hideous Lepage; and the romance between Eugène Saint-Céran and Amand's daughter, Amélie, which ends happily when the former graduates as a doctor and is able to bribe the previously obstinate father to consent to the marriage. The murder, and the story of Amand's search for the elusive formula for gold, were both based on real people and events in the Saint-Jean-Port-Joli region south-east of Quebec City.

According to André Senécal, this Gothic work achieves some unity 'at the level of its moral discourse'. He sees de Gaspé, the son of a penurious aristocrat, reflecting the unease of his social stratum before the growing materialism of an emergent capitalism, but not without ambiguity. Thus, for Senécal, what ties this loose work together is the thirst for gold. Indeed, in addition to Amand, who dreams of gilded treasure, there is Lepage, who kills for a pittance, and the central figure of a folk legend, Rose Latulipe, who, enticed by luxury, abandons her fiancé for an elegant gentleman (the devil in disguise). According to the misogynist Saint-Céran, the author's *alter ego*, women, those 'merchants of emotions', learn to flaunt their charms 'before those who have gold . . . even if they are degenerates'. Yet, having made money himself while seemingly condemning an acquisitive society, he says of his future father-in-law: 'He must be as poor as a churchmouse. I'll offer him some money and he won't be able to resist', thus preparing the 'purchase' of his betrothed.

Unfortunately the version of *L'Influence d'un livre* that most Quebec readers would know was that of the 'edited' second edition of 1864, which was revised by Casgrain and reprinted several times subsequently, with the good abbé, holder of the copyright, making a tidy sum, especially from the school market for which he was responsible. The 1968 edition, the first since 1885, is a facsimile copy of Casgrain's expurgated text, in which the rather mild erotic references and the host of quotes of authors who, since the original edition, had incurred the wrath of the Church, were unceremoniously removed. The title was also changed to give less weight to the alchemist's manual, and now became *Le Chercheur de trésors ou L'Influence d'un livre*. (André Senécal's edition of 1984 is the first to reproduce the original text and title.)

The imitative Gothic form represented the first phase of the emergence of the novel genre in French Canada. By the mid-1840s it gave way to the *roman de la fidélité*, which would be dominant for about a hundred years. This principal mode imposed on writers the task of inspiring readers to safeguard the French language, and the customs, traditions, and faith of the French-Canadian nationality in accordance with the ideological drive for survival (*survivance*). Its main branch was the *roman du terroir*—the novel of the land. The other branch, the historical novel, would appear later in the nineteenth century and also have a long life. Its main thrust, as we shall see, was to turn its gaze backwards to the 'glories' of the French regime.

The *roman du terroir* was inaugurated by *La Terre paternelle* (1846), a short novel by **Patrice Lacombe** (1807-63), which preached the superior values of the agricultural vocation over life in the cities and in the lumber camps or in the fur trade. Chauvin *père* deeds his land to his eldest son, who mismanages it; he then takes it back, rents it to Anglos, fails in business, loses his farm and is forced to lead a poverty-stricken existence, with his son, in Montreal. Salvation comes, however, from a formerly wayward younger son who had escaped to the *pays d'en haut* (the fur-trading areas upstream on the Ottawa River) and now returns with money enough to buy back the farm, *la terre paternelle*.

Both here and in *Charles Guérin: Roman de moeurs canadiennes* (1853), by **P.-J.-O. Chauveau** (1820-90), an inherited patrimony is in danger of falling into the hands of the *étrangers*—the *Anglais*, clearly named in Lacombe's work and referred to in a veiled way in *Charles Guérin*. It is the story of a family, headed by the widow Guérin, that nearly loses its property in the St Lawrence valley, owing to the schemes of Wagnaër, a Protestant from Guernsey, and his (Balzacian) corrupt lawyer. Their plot is thwarted by the return of one of the sons, Pierre, from Europe. He retrieves the heritage (as in *La Terre paternelle)* and creates an agricultural-industrial enterprise to keep young people from emigrating. Chauveau and Lacombe were the first novelists to transcribe phonetically many characteristic traits of Québécois popular speech (unfortunately, regional vocabulary was set off by italics) and to introduce genre scenes of typical Quebec rural life that would be imitated in the years to come.

Like *Charles Guérin*, the two-volume *Jean Rivard* (1862, 1864) by **Antoine Gérin-Lajoie** (1824-82), aimed to stop the mass exodus of French Canadians to the industrial towns of New England by urging settlement in as yet uninhabited regions of Quebec. Similarly to its predecessors but on a much larger scale, this epic 'novel' projected the establishment of networks of agricultural centres with seasonal, farm-related industries as an antidote to emigration and to the surplus of the so-called liberal professionals—priests, doctors, lawyers, and notaries. Like Lacombe and Chauveau, but with much more emphasis, Gérin-Lájoie counterpoised the rural and urban milieus, purporting to contrast the decadence of the city, which offered both superficial pleasures and profound misery, with the much simpler and healthier 'natural' environment of the countryside.

Gérin-Lajoie had already established a considerable reputation as the author of the song 'Un Canadien errant', about the exiled *Patriotes* of 1837, and of the historical play *Le Jeune Latour*, when his treatise-like *Jean Rivard* appeared in serial form for the first time (with its statistics, quotes from government reports, and copious economic, ethnographic, and linguistic notes). This, his one and only work of fiction—whose two volumes are subtitled *Le Défricheur* (The Pioneer), and *L'Économiste* (The Economist)—would become the most popular novel of the nineteenth century after *Les Anciens Canadiens*. Reprinted sixteen times up to 1958, it even ran in serial form in the Paris daily, *Le Monde*, some fifteen years after its first publication. The work would be called '*l'évangile rustique de la race*' (rustic gospel of the race) because of its preaching of the ideology of *agriculturisme*, the term coined by historian Michel Brunet for the doctrine of clerical and lay ideologues who mythified and glorified the forced retreat into the countryside of French-Canadian society following the Conquest. In epic style, using a military vocabulary (victory, conquest, siege, attack), Gérin-Lajoie tells the story of land-clearing in the Eastern Townships and the growth of his hero's '*petite république*', a nearly perfect utopian micro-society.

The first volume traces the herculean efforts of Jean Rivard and his loyal disciple, Pierre Gagnon, to clear the land and establish a foothold in the former wilderness. The second deals with the development of the colony, its growth in population and prosperity and the meteoric rise of the hero from simple pioneer to mayor, justice of the peace, militia major, and a revered member of the legislature. The colony grows into Rivardville, with its own parish and school board. The city-country dichotomy is articulated through the correspondence between Rivard and his longtime friend Gustave Charmenil, who is obliged to eke out a living as copyist and translator in Montreal, all the while commenting on the striking contrasts between his dismal life and the heroic feats of Rivard and his followers. Jean Rivard and the parish priest, Octave Doucet, whose name combines echoes of classical grandeur with gentleness, are the pillars of the civil society in Rivardville. They are often found past midnight in the presbytery discussing theology and philosophy, or planning the future of their community in the more unlikely location of the Rivards' bedroom where the hero's wife, the perfect Louise, had long been asleep. Thus Gérin-Lajoie, a founding member and three-times president of the radical-liberal-nationalist Institut canadien de Montréal—a sort of people's university that was to fight clerical hegemony for several decades—forsakes his earlier forward-looking ideas by conforming to the dominant Church-directed vision of the traditional society and succumbs to the strong ideological pressures of his day. The 'ideal' village of Rivardville was not without its rich and poor, masters and servants, prosperity for some, and charity for others. Nevertheless *Jean Rivard*, and its utopia of colonization, would be a model for countless *romans du terroir* in ensuing decades. *Les Anciens Canadiens* (1863)/*Canadians of Old* by **Philippe Aubert de Gaspé** (1786-1871) was published one year after *Jean Rivard* appeared in serial form. If, in Réjean Beaudoin's words, *Jean Rivard* was a 'prospective' work, *Les Anciens Canadiens* was a 'retrospective' one, with its action beginning in 1757, three years before the defeat of the French in what was to become Canada. Its success was immediate and it has been republished at regular intervals ever since.

According to Maurice Lemire, the earliest francophone novels of Quebec, whether works of adventure or rural sketches, did not attract a large reading public, and this led to the urging by ideologues that writers turn to historical novels, in the wake of the great success of Sir Walter Scott. Starting in 1863, and for the next fifty years, the historical novel would thus outpace all other sub-genres in an effort to overcome the 'frivolity' of readers. Writers would fuse history and fiction in a 'heterogeneous amalgam, each element of which could be separated without affecting the whole' (Lemire). Abbé Casgrain not only called on Quebec's writers to prevent folk legends from disappearing; he also promoted the popularization of little-known historical episodes, while at the same time warning writers to avoid political discussions. Aubert de Gaspé certainly heeded the first two appeals, but he was also inspired by the historian François-Xavier Garneau, whose monumental *Histoire du Canada* (1845-8) had not only given the lie to Lord Durham's gratuitous labelling of the French Canadians as 'a people without a history and without a literature', but provided an impetus for the emergence of a distinct literature, ideology, and mythology in Quebec. As for Casgrain's admonition to eschew politics, we shall see that Aubert de Gaspé was far from compliant.

If *Jean Rivard* proposed a prospective utopia, *Les Anciens Canadiens* celebrated the 'Eden of New France', from the point of view of the author's own seigneurial class. Part I (six chapters) of this historical romance introduces two young friends with differing backgrounds, Jules d'Haberville and the Scot Archibald (Arché) de Locheill, along with the quaint folkloric discourse (again set off in italics) of the servant-storyteller José Dubé. The next five chapters present the idyllic setting of the d'Haberville manor at Saint-Jean-Port-Joli, with its social harmony, aristocratic generosity, and distinct mores. The final seven chapters deal with the British invasion, in which Jules and Arché are on opposite sides, and the attack on Quebec and its aftermath. Arché, now a British officer, is made to take part in the burning of the farms on the South Shore, including the d'Haberville manor. Nevertheless, after the war he helps the d'Haberville family and returns to live nearby.

With the impending defeat of New France, Aubert de Gaspé leaves his third-person narration and turns to a first-person Garneau-like call to the francophones to overcome the humiliation of being a conquered people. Through a series of twists and turns the narrator next praises the *Cession* for having saved New France from the 'horrors' of the French Revolution and its aftermath, then forecasts another hundred years of struggle to safeguard the francophone nationality after the first century (1763-1863) of 'perseverance'. (This curiously projected history to 1963, the year of the first acts of political violence by the FLQ and the establishment of the Royal Commission on Bilingualism and Biculturalism.) Now the narrator evokes the Latin proverb *Vae victis* (woe to the vanquished), mourning the fact that 'the losers are always in the wrong', for history registers only their defeat. He again picks up his reconciliation theme as he praises the armies of both combatants but not long afterwards evokes the fallen French soldiers, wondering whether, after their long sleep, they will still remember their adopted homeland, 'now under the yoke of the foreigner'. Another shift, however, refers to Christian soldiers pardoning their erstwhile enemies.

The third-last chapter (XVI), 'De Locheill et Blanche', is a key one. Blanche, the well-named d'Haberville daughter, whose inviolable purity is more a patriotic than a sexual quality, refuses irrevocably Arché's offer of marriage, interrupting the proposal 'as if a viper had bitten her', for she cannot wed 'one of the incendiaries' of her family home. Her firm resolution is summed up by 'the chasm between us that I will never cross.' She and Arché, though very fond of one another, will thus remain unmarried—and good friends—for the rest of their lives. This symbolic non-consummation is all the more striking because the recalcitrant M. d'Haberville has come to terms with the new governor, Sir Guy Carleton, and Jules marries 'a young English damsel of great beauty', and later has a son christened Arché d'Haberville after his godfather! One of the last scenes of the novel shows Blanche and Arché, her 'brother', now nearing sixty, playing chess, that game of imaginary war and conquest.

Thus throughout *Les Anciens Canadiens* there is a constant tension between attempts to fuse, on a symbolic plane, the two adversaries of the Seven Years' War, and the recurring intrusion of history, which keeps them apart. The Aubert de Gaspé family had established many matrimonial links with highly placed British figures, as had been advised by Mgr Briand, Bishop of Quebec, following the Conquest. Blanche herself approved of such alliances, although she refused to 'set an example after so many disasters'.

Aubert de Gaspé—because of his family's and his own failing fortune, especially after the end of seigneurial tenure in 1854 reduced his income, and possibly because of the strong opposition to Confederation among French Canadians at the time he was writing his book—was highly conscious of its political implications. The compensatory structure of Arché's remorse and consequent favours to the d'Habervilles, the marriage between Jules and *une Anglaise* and their symbolically named son, is exemplary of a widespread tendency in French-Canadian historical fiction analysed by Maurice Lemire, whereby authors 'resolve' in their imaginary universes insoluble problems of social reality. If Aubert de Gaspé does this, it is not without ambiguity, for underneath the supernatural elements, presages, dire predictions, tales of sorcerers, lively repartees, songs, and humour there runs through *Les Anciens Canadiens* a thread of hope mingled with fear for the future of the author's people.

*Angéline de Montbrun by **Laure Conan** (Félicité Angers, 1845-

1924) is like no other French-Canadian novel of its time. (It was first published in serial form between 1881 and 1882, and came out as a book in 1884.) This work by Quebec's first woman novelist delves into the mind of a young woman torn between the desire for love and the morbid attractiveness of self-abnegation preached by some of the leading clerical and lay (male) ideologues of her time. Although, after a long and bitter struggle, she succumbs to the latter, the thirst for life is powerful and resurgent. The first section is made up of thirty-one letters exchanged between the witty Mina Darville (writer of more than half of them), her brother Maurice, and her friend Emma S., who is about to enter a convent; only two are written, respectively, by M. de Montbrun, the heroine's father, and Angéline herself. Mina thus dominates the first section, and many commentators have probed the reasons for the title character's speaking here so rarely in her own voice. Patricia Smart, in her Governor General's Award-winning study, *Écrire dans la maison du père . . .* (1988)/*Writing in the Father's House*, and Jacques Allard and Maïr Verthuy, in brief texts written about the same time, all conclude that Angéline's near-absence in the first part, as a character speaking in her own name, reflects her status as an object being exchanged between two men, her father and her eventual fiancé, Maurice, to whom the heroine is certainly attracted. We read of the meeting and eventual engagement of the young couple, and of the growing affection of Mina for Angéline's father, the widower M. de Montbrun. A very brief second section, narrated in the third person, then recounts the death of the latter in a shooting accident, with the resulting prostration of Angéline and Mina's breaking with her carefree past to enter the Ursuline Convent. Angéline's weakened physical and mental health are the cause of a fall, and the consequent marring of her beauty. Deciding that Maurice is losing interest in her despite his vows of eternal love, Angéline breaks the engagement and returns his ring. She leaves Quebec City and goes back to Valriant, where she isolates herself, wearing a dark veil on the rare occasions when she leaves her father's home. As in classical tragedy, the most dramatic events are thus presented 'off stage', while their consequences will be examined subsequently.

The third and longest section, *'Feuilles détachées'* (random leaves), is composed of Angéline's journal entries over a period of a year and a half, plus a few letters written between herself and a missionary protégé of her father's, and finally an exchange of adieus between herself and her former betrothed. Here Angéline comes into her own for the first time. Smart and Allard have equated Angéline's now taking pen in hand and composing her journal with Laure Conan's writing the novel and breaking the silence of her sex in the literary arena of her day. It is in the journal, of course, that the heroine's emotional/moral struggle is played out before our eyes. Smart sees this conflict—which, she concedes, ends in the destruction of the 'subject'—as still being a significant one in that the heroine rejects traditional marriage based on superficial attraction and motherhood, choosing, on the positive side, to 'write' the text we are reading. Smart sees in the fragmented form of the work Laure Conan's response to the strictures of her time 'when the emergence of a unified point of view in opposition to the dominant ideology was impossible.'

One area Smart understates (except for reducing it to a patriarchal paradigm) is the relationship between Angéline and her father. Since the 1960s a number of critics have been drawn to what Charles ab der Halden, a French critic of the turn of the century, referred to as the 'excessive' love between father and daughter. In *Angéline* this is not a figment of the reader's imagination. Consider the following quotes: 'She lives in him somewhat as the saints live in God' (Maurice); 'Angéline is a child [she is 18] and I want her to remain a child as long as possible' (M. de Montbrun); 'You say that she will love you. I hope so, and perhaps she would already be doing so if she loved her father less' (Mina); 'That ardent tenderness absorbs her' (Mina); '. . . between me and Angéline there is a perfect give-and-take; and her unconditional attachment, her passionate tenderness would make me the happiest of men if only I thought less often about the extent of her suffering, were I to die' (M. de Montbrun); 'In what a delicious union we lived together!' (Angéline). Maurice speaks of Angéline's 'cult' for her father, and in fact, when she returns to Valriant, she will write her journal in her father's study while often gazing ecstatically at his portrait.

Roger Le Moine and others have brought to light a real love relationship between Félicité Angers and Pierre-Alexis Tremblay, which was broken by the latter's lay vows of chastity, but they have not clarified the importance of this romance for an understanding of *Angéline de Montbrun*, and especially of the relationship between father and daughter in the novel. One has to agree with Patricia Smart that the heroine's 'rejection of happiness and life, but also her rejection of marriage, of men . . . is as ambiguous as the novel in its entirety.'

Although abbé Casgrain lauded *Les Anciens Canadiens* because he felt it responded to his call to writers to draw on legends and historical subjects, the ubiquitous cleric not only gave *Angéline de Montbrun* high praise, but also agreed to write the preface, in which he said that one takes leave of this novel 'as one would leave a church, with one's eyes on heaven, a prayer on one's lips, one's soul full of clarity and one's clothes fragrant with incense.' For a long time, in fact, this was the generally held view of the work, which approved its Christian resignation and the renunciation of earthly values following the heroine's facial disfigurement and subsequent broken engagement. But during the past thirty years critics have found many more troubling echoes in this complex novel, describing it as 'ambiguous', 'ambivalent', and 'enigmatic'. Almost all have agreed, however, on its importance as the first psychological novel of French Canada—or of Canada in general. It is the most important francophone work of fiction of the nineteenth century and one of the most commented on and analysed novels of the Quebec corpus. Although nearly every year brings longer or shorter studies of this work, it is certain that the critics have by no means exhausted the material and that more studies and insights into it will be forthcoming.

Laure Conan's attempt at a psychological presentation of character was exceptional. Most writers at the end of the nineteenth century, and well into the twentieth, perpetuated the novel of the land even after 1911, when Quebec's population was already almost evenly divided between town and country, and the irreversible trend to urbanization was accelerating. Most were lifeless problem novels, ever upholding the rural milieu as the cradle of French-Canadian spiritual values, and farming as the occupation closest to God.

Two novels that broke sharply with this trend, although in a quasi-clandestine way, were the underestimated *Marie Calumet* by **Rodolphe Girard** (1879-1956) and Albert Laberge's *La Scouine*. Both were the targets of fierce clerical attacks, the latter when chapters appeared in Montreal periodicals before it actually came out in a very small private edition and was sent by the author to friends. It would be many decades before these two 'sacrilegious' works entered the mainstream of literary circulation: Girard's in 1969 through a facsimile edition based on the original (the 1945 and 1973 editions being expurgated, and the 1977 English translation being based on the latter), and Laberge's in 1972.

*Marie Calumet (1904) has its origin in a scatological and salacious folksong of rural Quebec. At its centre is the priceless housekeeper of the title, who looks after the presbytery of *curé* Flavel, in the parish of Saint-Ildefonse (perhaps signifying *il défonce*—he breaks down doors or walls). Marie will be wooed by the priest's handyman, Narcisse, who eventually wins out over his rival, the beadle Zéphirin. The latter takes revenge on the wedding guests by putting a potent laxative into the main course of the feast, causing not only the newlyweds but also the village *élites*—the mayor, the doctor, the notary, the merchant, the church wardens— to rush to the *chalet d'aisance* (outhouse). In between the arrival of Marie in Saint-Ildefonse and her wedding celebration, the author has ample room to play on three elements of transgression: anti-clericalism, sensuality and sexual desire, and anti-agriculturalism.

The anti-clericalism of the novel is concentrated on the well-named Father Lefranc, who is a French-Canadian version of the *abbé galant* so frequently found in eighteenth-century French stories; on the already mentioned Father Flavel, priest of the parish in the centre of the action; and especially on 'Monseigneur', the otherwise unnamed diocesan bishop, whose ceremonial visit to Saint-Ildefonse is a high point of the novel's satire. Lefranc is especially attracted to Suzon, Father Flavel's pretty niece and servant-girl, and her charms bring shivers to Lefranc, who immediately shifts his thoughts to heaven 'without detaching his eyes from earth'. Besides his weakness for feminine pulchritude, Lefranc poses as a modern priest with liberal ideas who is also a shrewd speculator on the grain he receives in tithes.

Not only the ignorance but also the gluttony of the clergy are underlined by Girard as he desacralizes the clergy and brings it down to earth, to human size. In Chapter X, '*Ousqu' on va met' la sainte pisse à Monseigneur*?' (Where are we going to put Monseigneur's holy piss?), Girard is at his most irreverent. Marie Calumet swoons over the bishop's bedpan, exclaiming: 'A bishop's piss, there's something rare indeed!' The author goes on to stress the luxury of the bishop's apparel and accoutrements. In a close linking of the anticlerical and scatological themes, the so-called episcopal throne is described as 'one of those imposing patient's chairs with a very high back and a hole in the middle': the gold-coloured paper stars decorating the red cushion covering the hole stick to the cleric's posterior when he gets up to give the assembled crowd his blessing.

The agricultural vocation, held up by official ideologues as the foundation stone of French-Canadian civilization, also becomes the butt of Girard's pen. In mock-heroic style the author compares his simple rural characters, and the incidents involving them, to classical heroes and epic events. Complementary to this stylistic device is his emphasis on the peasants' ignorance, stupidity, superstition, and ugliness. Here Girard goes well beyond an attempt to deflate the reigning myths of the rustic idyll in projecting a misanthropic, and especially misogynistic, view of the human condition. Women are seen in turn as dried-up religious bigots, eccentric children, sexual objects, and archetypal scheming temptresses.

Girard's friend **Albert Laberge** (1877-1960) also demythified the countryside in *La Scouine* (1918)/*Bitter Bread*. The two launched a short-lived attack against the idealized novel of the land, and it was not until the late 1950s and the 1960s that neo-naturalism reappeared, some four decades after Laberge's novel, in works by Gérard Bessette, Marie-Claire Blais, and Roch Carrier.

Influenced by Balzac, Zola, and especially Maupassant, Laberge wrote *La Scouine* from 1895 to 1917, which may account for its compilation of brief scenes. As was the case with Girard, published chapters of the future novel were condemned by Archbishop Bruchési of Montreal as 'pornographic'.

La Scouine is made up of a series of tableaux of rural life in the Beauharnois area south of Montreal from 1853 until about the end of the century, loosely tied together by the tribulations of the Deschamps family, and the evolution of the life of one of the daughters: the cruel, misanthropic Paulima, nicknamed La Scouine, an onomatopoeic expression of the disgust of other characters over her malodorous bedwetting into adolescence. The story can be divided into four parts: from Paulima's birth to her sixteenth birthday; from her sister Caroline's marriage until the fateful fall of brother Charlot from the roof of a house he was building for a bride he would never have; the gradual breakdown of the Deschamps family through greed and violence; and the death of the father, Urgèle, and the mother Maço's move, with Paulima and Charlot, to a house next to the cemetery in her native village. The entire work is punctuated by an unvaried refrain—'the supper bread . . . heavy like sand, with the sour and bitter taste'—symbolizing not only the bread of the Deschamps's evening meal but their entire existence. The bread is ironically marked with the sign of the cross. In addition to the pessimistic fatalism of the work, and the loveless misery of the characters, there is a general assimilation of humans and animals, the stress being placed on purely biological behaviour. Also, Laberge compares the face of the parish priest to a piece of raw meat, an image that brings to mind paintings of Gustave Courbet (who died the year Laberge was born). Chronicling the breakdown of the rural family, and exposing human bestiality and the cheating of the poor and weak, *La Scouine* also offers this description of the aftermath of the physical attack on the father, Urgèle Deschamps, by one of his sons: 'Above the door, a scarlet Sacred Heart of Jesus, smiling with sweetness and serenity, contemplated the spectacle.' A rheumatic old man, Gagnier, praying for a cure, receives a splattering of mud as the bishop's carriage passes.

Critical evaluation of the novel's style and structure have ranged from near-total deprecation to exaggerated praise for an alleged fusion of form and content. (Gérard Tougas went so far as to call Laberge 'one of the greatest Canadian novelists', allotting him more space in his *Histoire de la littérature canadienne-française* than Gabrielle Roy!) Most critics have questioned the choice of the title, *La Scouine*, since other characters are equal in importance to Paulima. One could argue, though, that her perversity and arrested infantilism are symbolic of the harsh universe created by Laberge.

In any case, Albert Laberge is an important writer who was neglected by official literary history in Quebec until the 1960s. With the republication of *La Scouine* in 1972, his work was given its rightful place in spite of its rough-hewn character. The first critical edition of *La Scouine*, edited by Paul Wyczynski—who includes a long introduction and copious notes—appeared in 1986. A ballet, *La Scouine*, was created by Fernand Nault for Les Grands Ballets de Montréal in 1977.

While Laberge was nearing the completion of his attack on the most cherished foundations of traditional Quebec society—the Church, the family, the agricultural vocation—a French writer from Brittany, **Louis Hémon** (1880-1913), had arrived in Canada after several years in England, and would soon produce his **Maria Chapdelaine* (1916), an all-time bestseller and eventual model of the *roman de la fidélité*. Born in Brest in 1880, Hémon had already produced four novels and numerous articles on sports and open-air activities. In October 1911 he set out from Liverpool for Canada, hoping to observe the saga of the opening up of the West. He had left behind his actress companion, Lydia Kelley, and their two-year-old daughter. Hémon died when he was finally on his way westward after some twenty months in Quebec, run over by a train near Chapleau, Ontario, in July 1913. Most of that sojourn would find him in the Saguenay/Lac Saint-Jean area of northern Quebec, the novel's locale, where he worked on a farm and in various construction gangs. His famous novel was typed after-hours in a Montreal office and mailed to the Paris daily, *Le Temps*, exactly two weeks before his death.

About a year and a half earlier Hémon had sent the French publisher, Grasset, a journal kept during his Atlantic crossing. Usually referred to as *Au pays de Québec*, and originally printed in a small private edition, this short diary was renamed *Itinéraire de Liverpool à Québec* and republished in Brittany in 1985. It is fascinating to see Hémon anticipating the ideological *dénouement* he would give *Maria Chapdelaine* some two years later. The journal's undated entries show him forming many a key motif of his novel-to-be before he even set foot on Canadian soil—or shortly after, in the streets of old Quebec City. From the very first pages the harsh climate of Quebec is referred to in such expressions as '*le froid homicide*' (murderous cold). But he also attributes heroic proportions to Quebec, sketching elements of a 'New World' cult. The new land is already marked for him by a 'moving grandeur' shortly after his departure from Liverpool by boat, and the St Lawrence is given a symbolic moral quality as a 'river of liberty', running through a land barely scratched by human hands and far superior to the 'servile, humiliated waterways that traverse formerly great cities' in Europe.

Most striking is the germ of the much-commented-upon mysterious voices, which Hémon's love-pained and grieving Maria hears in the still of the night in the novel's critical second-last chapter. In the diary, Hémon especially stresses the resistance to change, and the perseverance, of the French Canadians—a theme that will later be at the heart of '*la voix du Québec*' that will irrevocably decide Maria's future as a farmer's wife who resists the temptation of fleeing the familiar sombre landscape for the bright lights and wooden sidewalks of life with Lorenzo Suprenant in Lowell, Massachusetts. In his journal notation of his wanderings through Quebec City, Hémon underlines the durability of the French fact in North America and the heroic resistance of the people of French origin to Anglo-Canadian and American pressures. He uses words like '*témoigne*' (bears witness) and '*témoignage*' (testimony), '*les voix des cloches*' (voices of the church bells), and generalizations like '*Québec n'a rien appris et rien oublié*' (Quebec has learned nothing and forgotten nothing), which will appear literally or in recognizable variations in Chapter

XV of the novel in the passage describing 'the voice of Quebec'. Clearly his attraction to the 'New World' was a by-product of his rejection of the 'artificiality of great modern cities' like Paris, where he had studied, and, in general, France's 'refined civilization, too far removed from nature' (Gérard Tougas).

A fellow-passenger on the Atlantic crossing, the Breton priest Jean-Marie Leventoux, described for Hémon the 'glories' of the colonization movement in the region where Hémon would end up and place the action of his work—thus diverting him from his intention to go immediately to the Prairies. In the region of Péribonka, the Chapdelaine family of eight lives on an isolated farm surrounded by the dark, threatening forest and there clears the land through ceaseless physical effort. The father, Samuel, was, like Hémon, a restless adventurer, who no sooner cleared one plot than he sought a new frontier to start all over again, while Laura, the mother, dreamed of living in the more established parishes. The two older sons worked in lumber camps in the winter, while Maria and the younger children stayed at home.

More representative of the spirit of adventure than Samuel is François Paradis, who sells his father's land after the latter's death and continues to work in lumber camps, as a trapper and guide, and as a trader with the Indians on an equal-to-equal basis in the area even further north than Péribonka. Maria and he fall in love and become secretly engaged, but the 'foolhardy' youth dies in a snowstorm in the middle of the novel when he leaves his lumber-camp and sets out to catch the train to see his beloved during the winter holiday. The author could not keep François—a potential agent of disequilibrium—alive and at the same time conclude the novel in the mystical and conformist manner he chose. (The surname of François Paradis suggests his other-worldliness.) Thus the sentimental choices of Maria are closely related to ideological ones. Lorenzo Surprenant, he of the exotic first name who entices Maria with the pleasant 'surprises' she will have living in his Massachusetts textile town, will have to be rejected, and thus disappears from the novel (like François), while Eutrope Gagnon, the stolid, superstitious neighbour of the Chapdelaines—whose first name, etymologically, means 'the right turn'—will end up the 'winner'.

In the brief last chapter—after her true love, François, and then her mother, had died—Maria tells Eutrope that she will marry him in a year's time. While she kept a vigil beside her mother's corpse, mysterious voices came to her in the night: the first, evoking the miracles of nature on the land; the second, the French heritage; and the third, the 'voice of Quebec'—half-way between a woman's song and a priest's sermon, according to Hémon, stressing the abiding qualities of the French-Canadian people and preaching fidelity to its heritage. 'In the land of Quebec, nothing must die, and nothing must change . . .' These voices had told her to stay.

It was these final pages, coupled with his death in Canada in 1913, that associated Hémon irrevocably with the right-wing nationalist cause in French Canada. The voice of Quebec—the strongest of the three voices heard by Maria, with its insistence that 'our faith, our language, our virtues and even our weaknesses become sacred, intangible things which must remain until the very end'—would strongly influence conservative writers in Quebec, whose selective memory isolated this admittedly important element of the novel. In this way, despite the novel's anti-clericalism and mockery of the French-Canadian worship of the '*enfant Jésus*', Louis Hémon, the unstable wanderer and religious skeptic, was transformed into the creator of a 'Catholic masterpiece'. It would take until the 1950s for the 'myth of Maria Chapdelaine' to die, when André Laurendeau and other Quebec commentators cried 'Halt!' to the enduring insistence that contemporary Quebec could still be read in the pages of this work.

The first reactions to *Maria Chapdelaine* in the Saguenay/Lac Saint-Jean area of the novel's setting, and elsewhere in Quebec, were rather negative. (A statue of Hémon was tossed into the Péribonka River, clerics fulminated against the author, who didn't go to Mass, and bookstores refused to handle the work.) But gradually a cult developed around the book and its author, with pilgrimages to the sites of the novel and other like activities on both sides of the Atlantic. Even though the first criticisms of its portrayal of pioneer farmers and its primitive Catholicism evoked anger, the novel had many imitators (Damase Potvin, Harry Bernard, Adélard

Dugré, et al.), as well as powerful defenders, like the future Cardinal Villeneuve, Mgr Camille Roy, and **Lionel Groulx** (1878-1967), founder and editor of *L'Action française*.

Groulx was a right-wing nationalist historian who embraced corporatism and anti-Semitism, and between the wars praised fascist dictators in Europe, arguing that Canada, too, needed a '*chef national*'. His novel, *L'Appel de la race* (1922)/*The Iron Wedge*, is probably the best-known work to have drawn its Manichean inspiration from Jules-Paul Tardivel's much earlier *Pour la patrie*, and probably from the 'voices' of *Maria Chapdelaine*. These had indiscriminately characterized '*étrangers*' and '*barbares*' (the anglophones) as having seized almost all the wealth of the country at the expense of the francophones. In his extremely didactic, melodramatic, and often tedious novel, Groulx seized upon the just struggle of Franco-Ontarians against the infamous Regulation 17—which, for some fourteen years, had severely restricted the use of French in the so-called bilingual schools of their province in order to promote ideas of ethnic determinism based on the racist ideas of Gustave Le Bon's *Lois psychologiques de l'évolution des peuples*. His hero, the anglicized lawyer and later parliamentarian, Jules de Lantagnac—who eventually becomes the leader of the Franco-Ontarian cause in the House of Commons after a pilgrimage to his native village in Quebec and to the tombs of his ancestors—declares: 'I have retrieved the soul of a sensitive, sentimental race, of an ordered essence, magnetized from above.' (Groulx's protagonist, in fact, reiterates what abbé Casgrain had written more than half-a-century earlier about the so-called 'essences' of the two peoples.) In contrast to these 'French' values, are the equally stereotyped 'sickly imprecision . . . jumbled thinking . . . and incoherence of the intellectual personality' attributed to the 'English'.

A quarter of a century earlier **Jules-Paul Tardivel** (1851-1905) had published his futuristic novel *Pour la patrie* (1895)/*For My Country*, a much more pronounced work of religious nationalism that led to his being called in recent times the father of Quebec independence. Projected into 1945-6, it contains miracles and crucial conversions to Catholicism that thwart a plan of the anglophone élite and francophone (mostly continental French) Freemasons in and around the federal government to impose a legislative union on Quebec with the rest of Canada and thus wipe out Quebec's unique character and religious values. As a result of the direct intervention of St Joseph, the République de Nouvelle France is established. As in Groulx's work, the victorious alliance is made up of clerics and lay leaders, although, unlike *L'Appel de la race*, the Tardivel novel also includes anglophone allies among its protagonists.

Marcel Faure (1922), by the journalist **Jean-Charles Harvey** (1891-1967), appeared in the same year as Groulx's novel and embraced the nationalist corporatism that the historian was promoting in *L'Action française*. It proposed the formation of a French-Canadian steel company to compete with Anglo-American businesses, and flayed British 'colonialists' and American 'invaders'. Harvey's *Les Demi-civilisés* (1934)/*Fear's Folly* anticipated the thrust of the Quiet Revolution by a quarter of a century in its severe criticism of Quebec society. The book cost him his job as editor-in-chief of the Quebec City daily, *Le Soleil*. Strongly anticlerical, its targets included educational institutions, restrictions on freedom of speech and artistic expression, and sexual taboos. The rhetorical dialogue, and a spectacular but unbelievable *dénouement*, weaken the work. But in spite of a persistent élitism, it has a prominent place in the history of ideas in Quebec.

La Chesnaie (1942), by **Rex Desmarchais** (1908-74), the action of which takes place in the years preceding the Second World War, is one of the last examples of the Manichean, chauvinist current of the *roman de la fidélité*. It recounts the failure of two French-Canadian intellectuals to create an independent, fascist-like state in Quebec through their 'Secret Dictatorial Society'.

The last outstanding work of *fidélité* was *Menaud, maître-draveur*/*Master of the River* by the priest **Félix-Antoine Savard** (1896-1982). It was published in 1937 (exactly one hundred years after *L'Influence d'un livre*) in the first of three versions, the last one in 1964. Menaud is an old log-driver in Charlevoix county who is inspired by these words from *Maria Chapdelaine*: 'We came three hundred years ago and we remained . . . Around us arrive foreigners whom we choose to call barbarians! They seized most of the power! They acquired almost all the wealth.' He suffers the drowning of his son Joson in a log-jam, and the failure of an attempt to oppose the 'foreigners', and while nearly perishing in a snowstorm, retreats into madness.

The rhythmic echoing of Hémon's *voix du Québec*—with stress on the timelessness and unchangeability of Quebec, its cult of the ancestors, its mystical link between nature and the 'chosen people', and its prophetic and epic dreams—makes *Menaud* a model of the novel of combat for the survival of a traditional culture—as does its vocabulary, deeply marked not only by colourful regionalisms, but also by emotional words of the nationalist lexicon like 'race', 'destiny', and 'blood'. Combined with these idealistic elements are such realistic ones as the physical misery and dangers faced by the log-drivers, their meagre pay, and the need for the anglophone company engineer to use an interpreter when offering to hire Menaud to head a logging expedition. The mountain, a sort of feudal common where Menaud has his hunting cabin, is leased by the ever-anonymous company, which chases the old logger away and makes the suitor of his daughter Marie— the devil-like Délié (the nimble one, but literally the untied, unattached one)—guardian of the domain about to be turned into a hydro-electric project. Thus the mountain is both symbol and microcosm of a vaster socio-cultural conflict, with roots in the reality of economic and cultural alienation. There is here what Hémon called in *Maria Chapdelaine* 'the eternal misunderstanding between the two races: the pioneers and the sedentary folk', between those peasants 'who on the new land transplanted their ideal of order and immobile tranquillity, and those other peasants in whom the vast, wild land awoke a distant atavism of wandering and adventure.' In Savard's novel this conflict, often found in French-Canadian literature, is epitomized by the loggers, headed by Menaud—with their open, free, linear thrust along rivers, over mountains, and through woods—and by farmers, like Josime, who are hemmed in behind their fences and constantly move about in circles or squares. In *Maria Chapdelaine* the forest is constantly seen as a threat, described always in sombre, hostile, inhuman terms, while high value is placed on its reduction and clearing. In *Menaud*, on the other hand, the forest (associated with the mountain) is the sphere of freedom, contrasted with the farm homes 'where one chokes', and tree images abound to emphasize the virtues of the strong and sinewy loggers.

In *Menaud*, however, the romantic sub-plot sharpens the ideological struggle in comparison with Hémon's work, for it pits the treacherous Délié against the faithful Lucon, the eventual winner of Marie's heart. Marie's shift from her dream of 'egotistical' security on the soil to a larger vision embracing 'the entire land' is, however, shrouded by Menaud's 'immense desert of madness'. His friend Josime's words, which conclude the novel—'This is not ordinary madness! Something tells me that it's a warning'—mean that the old logger's isolated battle to unite his folk against the endless encroachments of the '*étrangers*' is doomed to failure and dementia, and that an entire era and way of life were inexorably coming to an end. Thus the defeat of Menaud following the death of his son—like that of François Paradis—becomes a harsh blow to nature in favour of culture, in this case the agriculturalist, right-wing nationalist ideology. Similarly, erotic desire, also linked to nature, is fundamentally eliminated in both works, a fallen victim to a metaphysical, abstract '*héritage*'.

2

THE MODERN NOVEL:
1938-1959

Even before Menaud's madness signalled the growing crisis of the *roman de la fidélité*, arising from a society's crisis, there were signs that the persistent idealization of the land and of traditional values was coming under increasing, if as yet marginalized, criticism. As early as 1918 the short-lived magazine *Le Nigog*, named for an Algonkian fishing-spear, aimed its barbs at exclusive regionalism in all art forms, stressing instead total liberty for the artist in the choice of subject-matter and the importance of aesthetic concerns. Robert de Roquebrune, one of the founder-editors, declared: 'Let them leave us alone with their Champlain, *habitants* and native soil.' Another *Nigog* collaborator, painter Adrien Hébert, would be one of the first artists to depict urban and industrial Montreal, decades before writers turned to these subjects.

Accomplished French-born writers who, like Louis Hémon, fled what they saw as a stagnant and lifeless European civilization, sketched sharply the harshness of the Canadian North, and the desperate struggle of the colonist to clear the land, whatever may have been their ideological intention. Thus **Marie LeFranc** (1879-1964)—born in Brittany, like Hémon—in *La Rivière solitaire* (1934) painted a grim picture of unemployed workers from the cities answering the call of lay and clerical nationalists to create new farm colonies in the distant Témiscamingue area of northwest Quebec.

La Forêt (1934)/*The Forest* by **Georges Bugnet** (1879-1981), an ex-seminarian who was born in Burgundy, depicted the unsuccessful three-year battle of a young French couple—a journalist and a woman from a well-to-do family—to clear a homestead north of Edmonton, in a landscape described as 'that inhumane country', in the early years of this century. It portrays the brutalization of the pioneer, the progressive distancing of the spouses one from the other and their eventual decision to give up the land and move to Edmonton, admitting defeat. The accumulated sufferings of Roger and Louise are so overwhelming that they probably explain the cool reception given to the novel during the heyday of the colonization movement. In a less-polished earlier novel, *Nipsya* (1924), Bugnet's religious inclination is much more manifest. While purporting to show sympathy for the cause of Riel and the Northwest Rebellion through the eyes of the young Métis woman of the title (Cree for willow), he in fact denigrates the native mores and religion in favour of Catholicism and European culture, mainly through his spokesman, Vital Lajeunesse, a converted Métis. Natives and Métis are also present in **Maurice Constantin-Weyer**'s *Un homme se penche sur son passé* (1928)/*A Man Scans His Past*, which won the Prix Goncourt. The author (1881-1961) described his work as 'a poem of human will confronting a hostile nature'—a theme common to many works of the French-born writers. The narrator, Monge, following a superhuman fur-gathering expedition that takes up a quarter of the book, exclaims: 'Nature . . . is a monster with bloodied claws.' Constantin-Weyer's depiction of natural surroundings is strikingly plastic, and his language full of brilliant metaphoric imagery and fantasy. While not dealing with agricultural colonization, this novel's portrayal of ruthless nature dovetails with the works of the other French writers mentioned above.

Native-born authors also turned away from the rural idyll. *Le Nigog* contributor Jean-Aubert Loranger (1896-1942) ironically titled his collection of short stories *À la recherche du régionalisme*: *Le Village* (1925); it exposed the brutishness and hypocrisy of a host of rural figures. But it was especially *Un homme et son péché* (1933)/*The Woman and the Miser*, by **Claude-Henri Grignon** (1894-1976), set in the heart of the Laurentian colonization region, that disturbed the tradition of the consecrated novel of the land. This work—on pathological avarice and sado-masochism, which has evoked a variety of interpretations from Freudian to socio-symbolic—is one of the greatest successes of Quebec publishing. There have been at least eight printings up to 1980, and radio and television adaptations that ran, respectively, twenty-three and eleven years on Radio-Canada; it also inspired two films. In its treatment of poverty, exploitation, and aberrant sexuality there are elements of realism that break with the previous models of the genre. There is originality, too, in the choice of its villain, a French-Canadian miser rather than the stereotyped Jew ('old man Shouffe, the oldest and richest Jew in the land', *Charles Guérin*, 1853) or the exploiter of British origin—who, according to Antoine Sirois, was the most common negative character in his sampling of some 900 Quebec novels. In Grignon's portrait of an archetypal fleecer, there are echoes of Molière and Balzac.

The nearly illiterate farmer and skinflint moneylender, forty-year-old Séraphin Poudrier, marries twenty-year-old Donalda Laloge, his 'wife-servant', deprives her of food, clothing, and love, and consequently ensures that she will remain childless and a slave whom he will drive to death within a year. Donalda, described by Father Raudin as a saint because of her submission to humiliation and suffering, dies almost resigned, after a long agony. In her delirium she cries out: 'They've killed me . . . Oh, mother!'

Poudrier's displaced sexuality turns lustily to gold, and the descriptions of his ecstatic contemplation of his liquid assets—through the use of words like 'paroxysm', 'caressing his balance sheet', 'currents of electrifying joy'—have been compared by critics to auto-erotic orgasms. (His first name, signifying angel, has become the popular Quebec term for a miser.) The self-centred Séraphin remains passive at the funeral mass and interment of Donalda, and soon forgets her and her 'expenses'. He returns to his 'bachelor' life, eating his buckwheat pancakes, bitter soup, and mouldy crusts of bread, but growing more and more paranoid, and eventually dying as he runs raving mad into his flaming home, hoping to save his ill-gotten hoard.

There is a certain absurd logic in Séraphin's becoming a sexual abstainer in his marriage after a single brutal penetration, given that sex was admitted by the dominant clerical ideology only for procreation and that he had already rejected children as financial 'burdens'. Here there is perhaps one reason for the priest's lack of intervention on behalf of Donalda. According to Jean Le Moyne in *Convergences* (1960), since the only sin in French Canada worthy of discussion was that of the flesh, and the miser was seemingly 'innocent' in that regard (yet sorely tempted by his cousin Alexis's daughter, who totally rejected his advances), his behaviour was 'irreproachable' in the eyes of the Church! Although an occasional cleric criticized the 'excessive carnality' of Grignon's novel, most found it to be 'in the great Catholic tradition'. One dissenting voice appeared regarding Donalda's 'model behaviour', that of Viviane Décary, writing in *Le Canada* in 1934. She congratulated the author for having lifted the veil on a hitherto taboo subject, 'the deprivation of the joys of physical love from which the majority of the women of our race suffer because of the ignorance, brutality or at the very least, the lack of refinement of their husbands.' Grignon did not contradict her publicly, but wrote in an unpublished text: '[Donalda] accepted every sacrifice because she was profoundly Christian.'

Clearly, while Grignon's novel, through its greater realism, broke with the idealization of agricultural life, its ideological thrust fully supported the dominant ideology. By blaming poverty and suffering on individuals like Poudrier, it turned readers' attention away from the colonization movement and the economic crises engendered by capitalism. By its idealization of the 'saint', Donalda, and her 'Christian resignation', it basically excused Séraphin's ruthless behaviour towards her, and condoned the shamefully inferior position of women. Also, by making Alexis the most positive character in the novel, indifferent to his own exploitation by his cousin, the author emphasized the unalterable alienation of the French-Canadian people and its powerlessness to change its socio-economic conditions.

Trente arpents (1938)/*Thirty Acres* by **Ringuet** (Dr Philippe Panneton, 1895-1960) marked the death of the *roman du terroir*. (Seven years later, Germaine Guèvremont's *Le Survenant* would signal a brief resurrection of the genre, but only to give it a somewhat more decent burial.) The title—descriptive, objective, abstract—not only explicitly refers to a common measure of farm holdings in the St Lawrence valley; its repetition also provides a rhythm that implicitly sums up the entire action of the novel. In the ascending thrust of the first two sections, 'Spring' and 'Summer'—where Euchariste Moisan savours a fistful of rich, black earth—the title reflects positively his possession as 'guardian of these thirty acres of land'. But already the narrator is uttering, here and there, some dire predictions, which will come to pass in the descending movement of the last two parts, 'Fall' and 'Winter'. When the political organizer, Willie Daviau, tells the farmers why theirs, among the varied occupations, is the only one that doesn't permit freedom of movement to the point of making possible their election to the legislature, the narrator explains: 'Without man the earth bears no fruits and that's what ties him to the land, making him a prisoner of thirty acres of earth.' A strong contrast is also made between Albert, the hired hand from France, free to pick up any day and move on, and the farmers of Saint-Jacques, 'riveted to their thirty acres of land.' When disasters begin to shake the veteran farmer, he cannot understand why the land is abandoning him, 'he who had never had a real fatherland other than these thirty acres of Laurentian loam.' Various forms of alienation crush Euchariste: the conscription crisis in the First World War, the judge and lawyers in a humiliating lawsuit over a neighbouring piece of land, the opposition of two of his sons, and finally when he is persuaded into involuntary exile with his favourite son, Ephrem, in White Falls, Massachusetts, where he becomes a cog in the industrial machine as nightwatchman at the municipal garage. There, unable to talk with anyone but his son—not even with Ephrem's family—or even to communicate with the 'monstrous herd' of trucks at the garage, at the primitive level he enjoyed with his cattle, life draws in on him. Fatalism dominates the novel. In his White Falls garage, his faculties declining, Euchariste opines that he had not yet resigned himself to the idea of never returning to Saint-Jacques. 'Things had decided for him . . . . '

There are other dimensions to *Trente arpents*. Unlike the traditional novel of *fidélité*, it portrays the departure of young and old as final, with no return of the prodigal son to save the family fortune. Ringuet writes of a time when both farm and factory are in a state of degeneration. The farmer is afflicted by avarice, ignorance, theft, humiliation; the city dweller suffers from layoffs, plant closures, separation from nature, marital infidelity, and economic and cultural alienation. While this creates a kind of balance, Ringuet leans somewhat more to the traditional side with regard to the city, seeing it as little more than a den of iniquity in his intimation that Moisan's daughter, Lucinda, has ended up as a prostitute in Montreal, and that his daughter-in-law Elsie and his cousin's wife, Grace, are archetypal urban temptresses.

At the same time Ringuet shows proto-feminist sympathies in his treatment of Alphonsine, Euchariste's wife. The narrator depicts her inner thoughts of dismay in a powerful under-statement—'she who was only the mother . . .'—when the priest and her husband decide on their own that her eldest, Oguinase, will pursue a religious vocation. In one of the novel's most emotional scenes, when the moment arrives for her son to leave for the seminary, Alphonsine's consternation is such that she squeezes her younger son, Étienne, until it hurts, as her husband and Oguinase drive off to town. Equally powerful is the scene in which Alphonsine, not yet forty, already feels worn-out after years of child-bearing and is on the verge of death after bringing her last infant into the world. Looking at her reflection in the nickel-plated mirror of the kitchen stove, she sees 'a woman with lacklustre hair and a dried-up face'. Thus the sacred institution of motherhood is here sharply questioned by the author. And the inferior position of women, he makes clear, is one willed by the Church.

Paradoxically Ringuet's novel, 'which forever extinguished the age-old myth and mystique of the land' (Réjean Robidoux), was itself the high point of the *roman du terroir* launched by *La Terre paternelle* in 1846. *Trente arpents* was the first creative work by a French Canadian to evoke interest in the major francophone centres of the world, beginning with Paris, where it was awarded two prizes by the Académie Française. It brought the novel genre to 'formal maturity', and came at the right moment 'for other themes to develop subsequently in a living relationship with a more up-to-date reality' (Robidoux).

In Ringuet's novel Albert—a French pacifist fleeing army service, turned farm worker—shows up at the Moisan household and stays a while, bringing his non-conformist habits and sensitivity to that closed society. He is a *survenant* (unannounced stranger) and through him Ringuet turns his critical gaze on aspects of the suspicious routine-ridden parish. Seven years later *Le Survenant* (1945), by **Germaine Guèvremont** (1893-1968), placed a similar, though more mysterious, outsider at the centre of her work and in so doing highlighted the doom of the *roman de la fidélité* and of the agriculturalist dream. (An English translation of *Le Survenant*, and its sequel *Marie-Didace*, was published in one volume as *The Outlander*.)

Le Survenant presents a farm family that has lived for six generations on the same soil on the Chenal du Moine in the Sorel region. Its lineage is threatened by the physical and moral weakness of Amable Beauchemin, childless son of the patriarch Didace, and Amable's frail, frightened wife Alphonsine. *Marie-Didace* (1947) is named for the sickly child Alphonsine gives birth to, on the same day as Amable dies in an industrial accident. By 1917, at the end of the second volume (the action of the first covers the years 1909-10), Marie-Didace and her guardian, Angélina Desmarais, friend of her now-dead mother, are all that remain of the Beauchemin legacy.

In the first chapter of *Le Survenant* we are told of the arrival of a strange, alluring, red-headed outsider with new ideas, a harbinger of things to come, who shakes the Beauchemin family and the self-assurance of the community before moving on. He is the mysterious, anonymous Venant, who, it is strongly intimated, is a descendant of the Petit (wanderer) branch of Didace's family and is thus like a new-found son for the suffering patriarch. Venant is robust, creative, an assiduous worker, and a captivating storyteller and singer at the nightly *veillées*. He is honest (he fills the woodbox to the top, unlike Amable), simple (he wears the same clothes to work as to church), a skilful player of the harmonium, and an amateur scientist (he reads the *Journal d'agriculture* and finds new ways to grow clover and strawberries). Accused by Amable of having every vice, Venant answers: 'I admit I have some, but I have no faults. Whereas you haven't a single vice but have every fault there is.' He preaches the ideal of giving, drawing the lesson that 'whatever one gives to others is never lost.' He is indeed a sort of ragged Christ—he wears a small worn crucifix from which Jesus hangs by one hand, and he is linked metaphorically to the Messiah. There is a troubling love theme in the novel. Venant openly celebrates in words human, physical love, but he keeps a certain distance from women. To Angélina, who has fallen in love with him, he says that she should not tempt him with her offer of marriage, a home, and substantial property. At a final *veillée* he pulls his chair out of the circle (symbolizing the endless routine and prejudice of the community), bringing a sudden end to the evening, and departs—taking up his linear course, free of constraints and obligations.

In the first version of the novel, Guèvremont strongly intimated that Venant was a married amnesiac of French-English descent, who had disappeared from Quebec City some eight years earlier. In her will, however, she stipulated that this reference be excised in all subsequent printings, and this was done. Did she mean to suggest that this 'superior' being resulted from a fusion of the two founding peoples? Or perhaps she wanted to say that the modernization of Quebec could only be accomplished by 'outsiders'.

Richly detailed in its evocation of a traditional south-shore St Lawrence community, Guèvremont's novel has a more gentle, sympathetic tonality than Ringuet's as each author contemplates the demise of a longlasting way of life, but they arrived at the same point: with *Trente arpents*, writes René Dionne, 'the rural novel died; *Le Survenant* . . . will see only momentary poetic resurgence.'

In 1945, the same year that *Le Survenant* appeared, Gabrielle Roy's classic of social realism, *Bonheur d'occasion*—preceded the year before by Roger Lemelin's *Au pied de la pente douce*—finally brought the Québécois novel to the teeming working-class districts of Montreal's Saint-Henri and of Saint-Sauveur in Quebec City's Lower Town respectively. These were the first Quebec novels to put workers at the heart of the action.

Roger Lemelin (b. 1919) wrote a sort of trilogy by following *Au pied de la pente douce* (1944)/*The Town Below* with *Les Plouffe* (1948)/*The Plouffe Family* and *Pierre le magnifique* (1952)/*In Quest of Splendour.* Himself a product of Quebec City's Lower Town, he created a fictional universe with one major theme: the inability of gifted youth from the poor districts of the provincial capital to climb the staircases leading to Upper Town and carve out a prosperous and creative secular career there. (After a hiatus of thirty years, Lemelin also produced a much inferior work, *Le Crime d'Ovide Plouffe* (1982)/*The Crime of Ovid Plouffe*, a supposed sequel to *Les Plouffe*.)

In Lemelin's first novel two adolescent friends are in the forefront: the aggressive would-be writer Denis Boucher and Jean Colin, an occasional factory hand who supplements his meagre income by selling worm bait. Denis and Jean belong to the younger wing of the 'Mulots' (field-mice) clan, the poorest folk in the district, while their more regularly employed, more pretentious neighbours are called the 'Soyeux' (silky ones). At the novel's end both Jean and Denis's brother are dead, yet Denis, despite his ambivalence about his area—a mixture of belonging and shame— decides to stay in Saint-Sauveur. In a striking parallel with the opening pages of the novel, a younger group of 'Mulots' tumbles down the *pente douce* (gentle slope) with stolen apples and takes refuge in Jean's funeral procession, just as Denis and his gang had fled the police with their illicit pickings from the Dominican monastery. Besides the illness, poverty, and unemployment that plague Saint-Sauveur, rats and ants infest the area, which Denis calls a '*foire du ridicule*' (ridiculous fair). The static nature of life there is evident in the title, which also stresses the literal and figurative inferiority of the inhabitants, who are likened to moles.

Members of the clergy are generally satirized in the work through the comic names of the priest, Father Folbèche (mad spade), and his assistants the abbés Chaton (pussy willow) and Trinchu (fallen train). Only the Mulots' 'own' *vicaire,* Father Bongrain, escapes a pejorative label. The Church is ridiculed, too, for its obsession with a non-existent 'Communist' plot in the parish, and for Father Folbèche's great skills at wiping out the debt in record time, despite the indigence of his flock. Symbolically, the romantic rendezvous between Denis and his girl-friend Lise takes place amidst the ruins of the old church building. The alienation of the milieu is summarized in the phrase *'un peuple sans drapeau'* (a people without a flag), which Lemelin repeats in *Les Plouffe*, and in the description in the latter book of the Saint-Sauveur area as *'le cimetière des rêves de toute une classe'* (cemetery of the dreams of an entire class). In *Les Plouffe* Denis is relegated to a minor role as a friend of the leather-cutter and would-be opera singer Ovide Plouffe. Emphasis is now on that family, the name of which resembles a sputtering wet firecracker. (The grandiose first names—Théophile, Joséphine, Ovide, Napoléon—are comically at odds with the family name.) Father Folbèche is still head of the parish and forms a 'couple', a consultative unit, with Joséphine Plouffe, the domineering mother. Most activities now take place *away* from the church, some even reaching into Upper Town locations like the baseball stadium, the site of the printers' strike against the hierarchy's organ, *L'Action chrétienne*; or the army recruiting offices near the Château Frontenac, where Ovide and his future wife, Rita, spend a social evening stuck behind a pillar, as 'befits' Lower Town folk. Their first sexual experimentation takes place on the hillside overlooking Lower Town, their backs to the Dominican monastery.

Lemelin is very sensitive in *Les Plouffe* to the increasing Americanization of Quebec, as seen in the baseball fever in the parish, the popularity of Bing Crosby songs, and the chewing-gum habit of Joséphine Plouffe. He was also one of the first Quebec writers to associate the Québécois with American blacks, two decades before Pierre Vallières's *Nègres blancs d'Amérique* (1968)/*White Niggers of America* appeared. The collective revolt of Théophile Plouffe and the other strikers against the hierarchy and the Duplessis regime also marks a significant first in the Québécois novel. Lemelin at one and the same time condemns corporatist and pro-fascist tendencies in Duplessis's Quebec, and shows sympathy for the consternation felt by thousands when Cardinal Villeneuve calls for total participation in the Second World War.

On the other hand, melodramatic incidents and authorial intervention are more frequent than in the first novel. Caricature abounds in the tics of the various characters. The fan-shaped story, built around each family member and spread over seven years, contrasts with the tight unity and concentration of *Au pied*. Yet *Les Plouffe* had the ingredients for a very successful television serial on both the French and English CBC networks from 1953 to 1959.

In *Pierre le magnifique*—set in 1949-50—Denis Boucher is even more marginalized than in *Les Plouffe*, living with his mistress, Fernande, in the Latin Quarter near the old site of Laval University. Pierre Boisjoly, a student priest and the main character, is spurred on by Denis to avenge his and Denis's heritage of poverty by trying to rise to the heights of political power. But Pierre fails in this, and in his attempt at a liaison with Fernande, and finally returns to the seminary. The novel again transposes elements of objective social history—the campaigns of the Union des Bûcherons for collective agreements in the lumber camps, Georges-Henri Lévesque's attempts to set up a social sciences faculty at Laval University in the face of Premier Duplessis's opposition—and combines these with unbelievable incidents and flat characters.

In spite of weaknesses, the novels of Lemelin display the verve, spontaneity, humour, and satire of a keen observer of French-Canadian life. In his own characteristic way he was, with Ringuet and Gabrielle Roy, an initiator of social realism in the Quebec novel. Like them, too, he anticipated major transformations of Quebec society that began with the Quiet Revolution.

With *Bonheur d'occasion* (1945)/*The Tin Flute* **Gabrielle Roy** (1909-83) wrote the most acclaimed and honoured Quebec literary work since *Maria Chapdelaine*. Though just as geographically concentrated as Lemelin's novels, it has a universal appeal that accounts for its translation into many languages. The comparative stature of the two writers is also evident from the continuous critical comment on Roy's work year in and year out, while Lemelin's novels have evoked sparse research during the past decades. (Gilles Carle's fine screen adaptation in 1981 of *Les Plouffe*, however, revived some interest in Lemelin. Unfortunately

Claude Fournier's 1983 film, *The Tin Flute*, distorted the main thrust of Roy's novel.)

Florentine Lacasse, a young waitress, tries desperately to escape the oppressive poverty of Saint-Henri in southwest Montreal by winning the affections of an ambitious engineer apprentice, the cynical Jean Lévesque. Her mother, Rose-Anna, is progressively overwhelmed by the problems of her large family and of her alienated ex-carpenter husband, the dreamer Azarius. Jean abandons Florentine after making her pregnant, and his friend Emmanuel, who loves her, marries her unaware of her predicament, before going off to war with Azarius and other former victims of the Depression. The Depression looms large, affecting young and old, with the Second World War intervening as an ironic 'salvation' for the idle hands of two generations, or spurring on opportunists like Jean to take advantage of arms production. After Emmanuel and Azarius enlist, Rose-Anna's family disintegrates, despite her heroic efforts. Daniel dies of leukemia, Philippe finds work in a munitions plant, and Yvonne plans to become a nun. Florentine, a mixture of frivolity and responsibility, is the economic mainstay of the destitute family to which she contributes a substantial part of her meagre earnings. Her convenient marriage to Emmanuel while carrying Jean's child is the main illustration of the French title (meaning second-hand, or occasional happiness), which applies to many of the other players. Azarius remains ever young, contemplating his unused hands that used to build houses, while his wife is already old in her early forties after twelve pregnancies. Florentine sees childbearing as a process of physical deformation and ugliness, and the 'couple' is a problematic entity, as in much of Roy's work.

Although cuts in the second and subsequent editions of *Bonheur d'occasion* somewhat weakened its impact, social protest against the capitalist system and its reliance on war to 'solve' the economic crisis are central to the novel. Through Emmanuel, Roy projects a post-war period in which social democracy will curb the profit-driven dominant forces.

Technique and artistry help to make *Bonheur d'occasion* a consummate work of literature. Roy achieved rare success in her creation of unforgettable characters with distinct voice modulations and varied levels of speech (including the unwittingly humorous deformation of place-names and institutions by Azarius and others); in her excellent dialogue and her rendering of characters' thoughts and feelings; and in creating highly charged scenes that would not be out of place on the stage, such as the confrontation between Florentine and Rose-Anna when the mother guesses that her daughter is pregnant but says nothing, and the tense moment on Florentine's wedding day when Rosa-Anna rejects her silent plea for support. When Roy occasionally links the fate of her characters with hundreds of anonymous figures on the streets of Saint-Henri, one is reminded of techniques used by Zola and Steinbeck to emphasize typical human qualities of the main players. Woven into the three-month period of the novel are recollections of the past—Rose-Anna's and Florentine's memories of their respective childhoods, for instance, and Rose-Anna's of her first meeting with Azarius. There are rhythmic devices, such as the repeated interplay of *autrefois* (then) and *aujourd'hui* (now) and the progressively more evident sights and sounds of the war invading Saint-Henri, until they climax at the end of the novel with the clatter of thousands of hobnailed boots at the soldiers' farewell at Windsor Station. The cinematic technique of the close-up renders eloquent Florentine's anaemic fingernail during a dinner-date with Jean and, earlier, her shaking knees as she waits in vain at the movie-theatre for him. Symbolic and poetic description is used effectively for the walls that surge surreally around Florentine as she walks through the Saint-Henri factory district; for her confusion between paper and real flowers and plants, contrasting growth and stultification; and for Daniel's coveted tin flute, which he finally receives shortly before his death.

Roy's second novel, *Alexandre Chenevert* (1954)/*The Cashier*, was an offshoot of the realistic approach of *Bonheur d'occasion*, but also reflected the existentialist 'threshold of expectation' that pervaded the literary scene in France around 1950, where Roy wrote the work, which she struggled with over several years. The hero is portrayed partly through his actions and partly through his thoughts, dreams, obsessions, and reveries conveyed by internal monologues. Chenevert is a typically harassed and alienated bank-teller—an Everyman of the metropolis, suffering from insecurity, ill health, and constant bombardment by contradictory media messages and solicitations. Unlike the characters of *Bonheur d'occasion*, who absorb daily the omnipresent English-language billboards and commercial trade names without reflecting on them, Chenevert is highly conscious of this key aspect of cultural alienation. (Roy thus anticipated the concerns of the younger writers of the 1960s and 1970s, and their preoccupation with language as a crystallization of the anxiety over cultural survival.) But he is also imbued with a deep, humanistic spirit and exemplifies '*l'immensité enfermée dans [une] petite vie*' (the tremendous scope contained in the life of a little man). Of the three parts of the novel, the first and last are centred in Montreal, while the middle section relates the teller's imposed vacation in the Laurentian countryside. The photographic realism of Roy's first work here gives way to a vaguer pattern of topographic reference. The street Alex lives on is never named; only his number, 8846, is given. And the mechanization of the city is seen, too, in the ciphers by which the various streetcar lines are designated and by the noisy adding machines of his workplace—a reference system that is in keeping with the universality of the main character and the existentialist and absurdist nature of much of the narrative.

Chenevert is described as '*le petit homme de la cage numéro deux*', working in one of five identical 'cages' at the bank. He sees life as a vicious circle: one had to keep on working (before Medicare) to earn enough money to buy medicine, thus assuring one's ability to go on with one's job! From the large indigent family of *Bonheur d'occasion*, the main social unit here is reduced to a mismatched lower-middle-class couple, and the focus is on one lonely individual. Not only do the Cheneverts barely communicate with one another; their daughter, Irène, is separated from her husband; and the bank manager, Emery Fontaine, and Chenevert's longtime co-worker Godias have only tenuous links with him. The general isolation of individuals is vividly illustrated when Chenevert says goodbye to his departing daughter at the bus depot and their words are drowned out by the revving of motors in a stench of carbon monoxide. Ironically, it is only when he is about to die, that Chenevert experiences some of the milk of human kindness for which he has always yearned and that he dreams will one day cover the globe. Chenevert's humanism is restricted to abstract beings suffering in distant parts of the world—he finds it difficult to relate to people around him. He dreams of escaping to a Polynesian island where, he believes, life will be simpler and more fulfilling.

His trip to a lakeside cabin near Saint-Donat gives him temporary solace and inner peace. A religious skeptic, he is almost ready to pardon God for the vast suffering of humankind. But in the end this philosophical voyage leaves him hungering for the anonymous throngs of the city and for newspapers from around the world. He is repelled by the ignorant selfishness of his rural hosts and angry at himself for having become engulfed in a river of forgetfulness at Lac Vert. In the middle of the Cold War, Chenevert longs for a day when atomic weapons will be destroyed, when peace and fraternity will rule the earth, and he envisions a world in which wealth will be used to better human life for all, rather than for the few. He grieves deeply over the assassination of Mahatma Gandhi and decides to fast in honour of the Indian pacifist, to the consternation of his wife.

Chenevert, a deistic humanist, is strongly critical of the Catholic Church's social role and rejects individual salvation. Shortly before his death from cancer, and uninhibited after taking painkilling drugs, he sacrilegiously inverts the God-human relationship by arguing with the hospital chaplain, the haggling Father Marchand, that if God had a heart as big as an ordinary mortal's, it would be a great thing. Nearly a decade before Vatican II, Roy's hero anticipates the *aggiornamento* of the Catholic Church, and even goes beyond it. Chenevert is a sort of secular Christ who boldly prefers everyday folk to the saints of the Church.

Through her concern with cultural alienation, her relentless questioning of the Church's social and temporal role, her ardent expression of the need for peace and understanding among the world's peoples, and her vision of the urgency of social reconstruction and reform, Gabrielle Roy anticipated the Quiet Revolution in her two Montreal novels and went considerably beyond its ideological confines. From the ironic theme of salvation through war that came to the poor of Saint-Henri, and the sombre clouds of the last page of her first novel, Roy shifted to the glimmer of hope contained in the life and death of her little teller, the echo of whose name resounded here and there in the city, outside the churches, after his death, and whose social philosophy was summed up in a short but meaningful sentence: '*Il éprouvait cependant qu'il y a quelque chose d'humiliant à être homme et à ne pas lutter contre le malheur.*' (He felt that there was something humiliating about being a man and not fighting against misfortune.)

While the socially committed novel continued to appear in works by **Jean-Jules Richard** (1911-75)—*Neuf jours de haine* (1948) and *Le Feu dans l'amiante* (1956), treating, respectively, the Normandy invasion and the 1949 Asbestos strike—and by **Pierre Gélinas** (b. 1925)—*Les Vivants, les morts et les autres* (1959), on various trade-union and radical political conflicts—it was generally relegated to a secondary rank, thanks to the strength of clerical domination of the literary institution (book publishing, newspaper criticism) and the influence of 'spiritualism' on journals like *Cité libre*, founded by Pierre Elliott Trudeau and others.

Thus, as Roy and Lemelin were moving the novel towards urban social reality, another major trend was beginning to emerge in the literary landscape. Catholic intellectuals grouped around the journal *La Relève* (later *La Nouvelle Relève*)—founded in 1934 by Robert Charbonneau and influenced by such French writers as Mauriac and Bernanos—began to create a sub-genre in the forties and fifties oriented towards internal spiritual yearning and personalist philosophy. It has been variously labelled the 'novel of psychological analysis', 'the novel of inner life', and more recently by Jacques Michon 'the novel of the moral dilemma', which he sees as the dominant approach in the 1950s. Michon speaks of a '*dispersion des normes*' in this type of novel, with the onus on the reader to take sides. Writers like Charbonneau, Robert Élie, André Giroux, and others reflected the malaise of Catholic intellectuals who, at one and the same time, felt disoriented in the atmosphere of religiosity and corrupt, reactionary politics during the years when Maurice Duplessis dominated public life in Quebec, while also rejecting radical political *engagement*. Suffering from a situation of *anomie*, they created heroes engaged in a frenzied search for new values in a world where the old ones are found to be inadequate. These new heroes desperately search for ideals, friendship, love—often failing in their quest, often resorting to suicide or murder to express their alienation.

Ils posséderont la terre (1943) and *Fontile* (1945) by **Robert Charbonneau** (1911-67), *Au-delà des visages* (1948) by **André Giroux** (1916-1977), and *La Fin des songes* (1950/*Farewell My Dreams* by **Robert Élie** (1915-73) all include vague elements of social criticism in an other-worldly atmosphere, and are usually schematic and arid in literary style—though their introspection, and internal movement back and forth in time, have been influential in the development of narrative technique.

André Langevin (b. 1927) is the most important novelist of psychological analysis and moral conflict. Although he did not come out of the Catholic intellectual tradition of *La Relève*, and was in fact strongly influenced by the existentialist current of Camus and Sartre in France, he is seen to have a number of points in common with the above writers, though he far surpassed them in aesthetic achievement and has been recognized as a towering figure in the evolution of the French-Canadian novel.

Langevin produced three novels in quick succession in the fifties. The first, *Évadé de la nuit* (1951), written when he was just twenty-four, is a didactic literary exercise, but already contains the essence of his world outlook: one of the characters speaks of human trajectories that never intersect, foreshadowing the parallelism of Langevin's outstanding *Poussière sur la ville* (1953), where the narrator, Alain, sees himself and his wife, Madeleine, as travellers along similarly distanced parallel paths. *Le Temps des hommes* (1956), the title of which is derived from Job's prayer, also treats the failure of the hero, the ex-priest Pierre Dupas, to commune with other human beings through love or compassion.

Langevin's heroes are concerned with God, a blind Providence, but as Jean-Charles Falardeau has said, nowhere is there such extreme solitude and distress as Langevin lays bare. The critic relates the title of *Poussière sur la ville/Dust Over the City* to the

Biblical 'dust to dust . . .', and stresses the central role played in the novel by the dust-laden atmosphere of the asbestos-mining town in Quebec where the action occurs. True to the novel of moral conflict, neither the province nor any real locality within it is ever expressly mentioned, although the fictional town of Macklin is modelled on Thetford Mines. Let us note the anglophone resonance of Macklin, with its main street, Green Avenue, and its Benson Mining Company. The anglophone mine-owners are absentee proprietors, whose presence is implicit in the above names, and in the habits of the local *notable*, department-store owner and financier Arthur Prévost (i.e. *prévaut*, prevails), who apes the supreme power-brokers. (Curiously, there is no mention of the Asbestos Strike of 1949, which, occurring four years before the novel appeared, is a landmark in the social evolution of Quebec.) Dr Alain Dubois struggles against the devastating discovery that Madeleine, his wife, has committed adultery with a truck-driver, Richard Hétu. Dubois gradually moves towards a feeling of pity as he witnesses the collapse of her liaison and becomes her 'ally against absurd cruelty', all the while being scorned by the town's *élites* for his 'outrageous' behaviour and, it is implied, by the workers who disdain the weak cuckold. The curé denounces him and moves quickly to arrange the engagement of Hétu and Prévost's niece. This provokes Madeleine's attempt to kill Hétu, and her subsequent suicide. Yet Alain—further devastated by his unfortunate operation on a child, and conscious of the tragic mechanism that ensnares human beings—is able, through his pity, 'to reach a state of relative calm, making it possible for him to endure the affront of which he is the victim. This attitude . . . makes of him a sort of secular saint . . . a formulation dear to Camus' (André Brochu). Alain's decision, after the tragic events, to stay in Macklin against all odds has been interpreted in various ways, but it is clear that his resolve to remain 'against the whole town' flows from his perception that everyone opposes him. There is, in fact, ample evidence to suggest that he also bears some responsibility for the perceived hostility on the part of the common folk through never seeing them as individuals. Significantly, it is only immediately before his decision to stay in Macklin that Alain utters the name of a patient for the first time: Marie Théroux is to have a baby, and the telephone rings to tell the doctor that the time has come. Thus is he encouraged to think that life must go on.

Yves Thériault (1915-83) had quite different literary preoccupations from the novelists just discussed. He was already an established writer in the 1950s following publication of a short-story collection *Contes pour un homme seul* (1944), two plays, and six novels. This first book already contains in its title the solitary hero, a recurring figure in his future novels; and the content, described by Maurice Emond as full of 'demented gestures, mutilations, murders, suicides—all this in a nightmarish atmosphere' presages the author's enduring *'primitivisme'* (Gérard Bessette) that set him apart from the main currents of post-war writing we have been examining, and that he pursued in his first novel *La Fille laide* (1950).

Two of Thériault's best-known novels, *Aaron* (1954) and **Agaguk* (1958), belong to this period. But because the latter is part of an 'Eskimo' trilogy with two other works published in 1969 and 1975 (*Tayaout, fils d'Agaguk* and *Agoak*), they will be discussed as a group in the next chapter. *Aaron* has been called 'one of Thériault's best novels, if not *the* best' (Renald Bérubé), and it is certainly admirably structured and written. (It is regrettable that copyright problems still prevent it from being translated into English.) From the very first page Thériault establishes the basic conflict between Moishe, an Orthodox Jewish immigrant tailor, and his grandson Aaron: the old man, with his other-worldly preoccupations, 'looking without seeing, hearing without understanding', and the boy, 'his eyes wide open, listening to the pulse of the feverish life outside which reached all the way to him.' The final chapter, when Aaron has changed his name and broken the family tradition of tailoring to enter the financial world, echoes the first (as Renald Bérubé has pointed out) by marking the victory of 'the sonorous new language of the century'; and there are other such symmetrical couplings. The characterization of Moishe is the outstanding achievement of *Aaron*, contradicting the title, through which Thériault sides with the rebel as was his habit. The author plays on the symbolic resonances of the Biblical names of the characters, and on the ironic role of Mount Royal, as compared to the mountain's sacred nature in Jewish history. Significantly, too, Thériault flayed 'Christian' anti-Semitism in this work through somewhat gauche authorial interventions. Some critics have rightly seen in *Aaron* a possible allegory of French-Canadian life, which Thériault vehemently denied. Nevertheless, the conflict between the new and the old, between a religion forged centuries ago and life in the modern metropolis, can also be interpreted as the very struggle that was rocking Quebec's religious and secular foundations in the post-Second World War period.

The sub-genre of the historical novel, a dominant mode in the nineteenth century, fell victim to social realism and psychological introspection. *Les Habits rouges* (1923) by **Robert de Roquebrune** (1889-1978) is an underestimated reconstruction of the 1837 Rebellion. But the only outstanding historical novel of the period under review is *Les Engagés du Grand Portage* (1938)/*The Making of Nicolas Montour* by **Léo-Paul Desrosiers** (1896-1967). It traces the rise of Nicolas Montour (my turn) to the heights of power in the North West Company at the beginning of the nineteenth century, after bitter struggles against all those who stood in his way. The malevolent Montour is pitted against Louison Turenne in a somewhat melodramatic manner. Although the work has great epic power and shines in the eloquent economy and liveliness of its writing through use of the historical present, Desroriers broke with tradition by creating a work in which the evil character is triumphant. The forces of good, rather than facing up to those of evil, refuse to sully themselves: rather than confront Montour, Turenne withdraws to his native village and takes up life again on the soil. Michelle Gélinas has called this novel both a work of 'resistance' to the traditional subservience of French Canadians to powerful anglophone economic interests, and one that is 'painful and pitiful, as is the literature of *survivance*, the daily bread of which is doubt, wariness, and resentment.' In opposition to popular myths of the North and the *voyageurs*, Desrosiers's novel—which won the Prix David jointly with Savard's *Menaud maître-draveur* in 1938 (in a certain sense it is in opposition to Savard's novel)—shows that the domination of the huge fur companies turned the Northwest into a 'new jungle', 'a frontier where mercantilism flouted all laws and values, and only profit counted' (Maurice Lemire). Montour exploits both *voyageurs* and Indians, the latter being robbed of their pelts and plied with brandy, and cynically marries a chief's daughter to further his personal cause. *Les Engagés*—by the sweep of its social canvas, by its breathtaking pace and immediacy of narration, and in the depiction of frenzied ambition and personal aggrandizement—has a permanent place in Quebec literature.

At the end of this period three writers—Gérard Bessette, Anne Hébert, and Marie-Claire Blais—wrote important first novels (*La Bagarre*, *Les Chambres de bois*, and *La Belle Bête*) that began their careers as novelists. These will be discussed in the next chapter with their subsequent works.

3

THE SIXTIES

In the reform movement of the 1960s that produced tremendous changes in every facet of Quebec life, the creative arts, including literature, were both catalysts of these transformations and by-products of them. As significant as the weakening of the Church by growing secularization and modernization was the change in self-image of the francophone majority of Quebec, which relatively quickly dropped the vague label 'French Canadian'—one that denoted an undistinguishable *minority* from coast-to-coast—for the term 'Québécois', which clearly signalled a *majority* in a precisely delimited area. This same central shift was also one away from a self-conception of the francophones as *individuals* to a new consciousness of themselves as a *collectivity*, a difference that is still very germane to the constitutional crisis that Canada and Quebec find themselves in it at this very moment.

The past three decades have seen a flowering and variegated enrichment of the novel as both an echo of, and a stimulus for, the changes of the Quiet Revolution. Like the period as a whole, the novel too gave vent to explosions of anger and violence through the literary language, syntax and formal structure, and thematic treatment. The predominance of first-person narration, which more and more replaced third-person omniscient storytelling, was perhaps the most obvious and understandable example of literary change, expressing not only the desire for more direct communication with the reader but also a new frankness.

Historical chance has decreed that the beginning of each of the three decades since 1960 marked an important moment in

Quebec's evolution. In 1960 the Union Nationale was swept out of office (and eventually into oblivion, after its last fling at power between 1966 to 1970) by Jean Lesage and the Parti Libéral, with its slogan of *Il faut que ça change* (Things Must Change). This led to a vast movement of reform and the official substitution of the term *État du Québec* for *Province de Québec*. The October Crisis of 1970 brought political violence to the Montreal region and nationwide (even world-wide) media attention. In 1980 the government of the Parti Québécois was defeated in its attempt to get public approval by referendum to negotiate sovereignty-association with the federal government. (The present decade began, too, with the failure of the Meech Lake Accord, and the Mohawk crisis, both of which have affected Quebec deeply.) As these key events have impinged on novel production, and on all aspects of Quebec socio-cultural life, it will be convenient to group the novels discussed within the above three time-slots, despite a certain element of arbitrariness in the procedure, since many authors span these divisions.

The 1960s saw the first emergence or maturation of Gérard Bessette, Claire Martin, Marie-Claire Blais, Jacques Ferron, Jacques Godbout, Hubert Aquin, and Réjean Ducharme; felt the shock-waves of the naturalistic/realistic writers associated with the political and cultural review *Parti pris* (founded in 1963 and published monthly)—Jacques Renaud, André Major, and Claude Jasmin; and saw the continuing production of Gabrielle Roy and Yves Thériault.

The first novel of **Gérard Bessette** (b. 1920), *La Bagarre* (1958)/ *The Brawl*, which appeared towards the end of the preceding decade, treats the 'two' lives of Jules Lebeuf—a failed university student, would-be novelist, and night-time streetcar sweeper—and is early evidence of the author's keen interest in social issues and in the variety of levels of spoken French. But Bessette would make his mark as a novelist of prime stature with *Le Libraire* (1960)/*Not for Every Eye* and *L'Incubation* (1965)/*Incubation*. The first of these has been characterized as an exemplary work marking the emergence of the individual word of the diarist-narrator against the monopoly of *la Parole*, held by the clergy, and pioneering the use of auto-referentiality and richly experimental self-expression that soon became a trend.

The satirical *Le Libraire* is made up entirely of the weekly journal notations of Hervé Jodoin, a clerk in a bookstore of a fictitious Quebec provincial town, Saint-Joachin. His entries, from 10 March to 10 May of an unspecified year, usually describe his daily routine—evenly divided between work, the tavern, and sleep—until a series of dramatic events intervenes, including a liaison with his landlady. Jodoin had quit his job as assistant master at a Catholic secondary school because of a poor salary and relegation to the lower grades. In his new post he is again in an uncreative job as a handler and seller, but not a reader, of books, though in his youth he was a '*dévoreur*' of literature and a member of the '*Cercle des amis du livre*'. After his employer tells him of a secret chamber or 'capharnaüm' where books on the Index are kept— books 'not for every eye'—and puts Jodoin in charge of selling them secretly (a task that excites him because it might give his life some meaning), Jodoin tricks his sanctimonious and hypocritical employer and the Saint-Joachin 'Jansenists' by diverting the for- bidden books from their hiding-place to Montreal, where he him- self will pocket the money from their sale. The projected end of Duplessis's infamous 'padlock law' is symbolized by Jodoin's removing and slipping into his pocket the padlock of the door to the 'capharnaüm' shortly before he leaves with the room's con- tents and heads for Montreal. There 'he will store speech' until his people in Saint-Joachin 'will be ready to welcome the new word' (Michel Bélair).

Jacques Godbout called Hervé Jodoin 'the first mythical Québécois, rather than French-Canadian character . . .' for his seemingly misanthropic and cynical, yet ultimately heroic, rejec- tion of his society's values. Jodoin reflects on many problems related to literature: reading, writing, the language of communica- tion, the system of book distribution, censorship, etc., all facets of what is now called the literary institution. And the supposed non-reader that Jodoin had become makes offhand references to Flaubert and Rousseau, cites Voltaire's real name, Arouet, and sells that writer's condemned volume (*L'Essai sur les moeurs*) to a student (thus creating a scandal) because he sees in the youth an image of himself a decade or two earlier. Flaubert is also implicitly present in the narrator's frequent rendering in quotes or italics of the hackneyed phrases of conventional 'wisdom' of his new milieu, recalling that author's glossary of just such phrases appended to his novel *Bouvard et Pécuchet*. The self-reflexivity of *Le Libraire* is also seen in the frequent references by the diarist-narrator to the act of writing.

In 1965—a boom year for Quebec writing, with major works by Aquin, Blais, Martin, Godbout, and Ferron—Bessette produced his highly polished, richly imaginative and moving stream-of-consciousness novel *L'Incubation*. According to the author the work grew out of a serious infection and partial paralysis that had almost killed him two years earlier, and left a mark of profound pessimism on him. Indeed, an ominous fatality hangs over the characters and the significantly named Narcotown of the setting (the slightly veiled Kingston, Ontario, where the author lives). The novel consists entirely of a long, one-paragraph internal monologue structured by the free association of ideas in the mind of the narrator, the library technician Lagarde, the only French-Canadian employee of the Sir Joshua Roseborough Memorial Library of Princess (read Queen's) University. The monologue is generated by the suicide of Antinéa (Néa), the wartime mistress of Lagarde's friend Gordon Blackwell, a French professor. News of the suicide, a traumatic event for the narrator, with whom Néa worked, comes in the form of a nocturnal telephone call from the old Vienna-born philologist Weingerter, Néa's landlord and another habitué of the library. It awakens Lagarde from a drunken stupor following a wild party he had attended with Blackwell and is recounted at the very end of the novel. Yet this end is, in fact, the beginning of the action, for the entire work constitutes the almost hallucinatory attempt by Lagarde to put together the pieces of the tragedy and discern his role as intermediary in it, friendly as he was with the above-mentioned characters as well as with Maggie, Blackwell's estranged wife. There is an uninterrupted flow of memories, recalled anecdotes related to the narrator by Blackwell and Weingerter, imagined variations or projections based on these, dreams and nightmares, disjointed strands of speech, and an explosion of neologistic creation.

The narrator occasionally reflects on his and Blackwell's deeply sombre view of the world, in which concepts like freedom, free will, civilization, and reality are treated skeptically. Most striking is a long passage in which their stark view of evolution suggests the futility of their humanoid ancestors' eventual verticality. Here Bessette's world-view is that human happiness, or even meaningful communication, is impossible. An implacable destiny entwines human beings in a series of labyrinths (i.e. the London Underground's bomb shelters, the stacks of the University library) from which there is no escape. Clearly one must agree with Glen Shortliffe, the translator, that with this work Bessette completed the shift begun in *Le Libraire* from social to metaphysical satire.

And yet there is in *L'Incubation* a certain nostalgia for the social comment that marked Bessette's beginnings as a novelist (in *La Bagarre* and *Les Pédagogues*, 1961). This is seen in the treatment of the grim Nazi epoch, and in one of the novel's memorable passages: the satirical allusions to the debate over the need for a distinct Canadian flag in the 1950s, revealing an underlying strain of Québécois nationalism.

Bessette's *L'Incubation* is a work of pessimistic humanism probably marked, as in *Le Libraire*, by the author's physical suffering as well as by the emotional scars he received during the Duplessis years when, as a brilliant graduate of the Université de Montréal, he was denied a teaching post at that institution because of his anti-clericalism. Against the certainties proffered by traditional ideologues, *L'Incubation* poses the quest for identity in ironic terms, characterized by the refrain *comment savoir* (how can one know?), a further skeptical variation of Jodoin's *peu importe* (who cares?), but is not without touches of social and political satire.

Critics usually accord to the first novel of **Jacques Godbout** (b. 1933), *L'Aquarium* (1962), the honour of being the pioneer work of fiction to break with linear time-schemes and unique omniscient third- or first-person narration. It is set in a vaguely eastern country where international technocrats vegetate during the rainy season in the Casa Occidentale, while young local revolutionaries prepare to overthrow a theocratic-feudal regime that may be a parallel for Quebec's during the Duplessis era. The work begins with a third-person narration to sketch the background, then shifts to first-person as the nameless narrator relates his liaison with the former mistress of a pro-revolutionary colleague who had been left to die by the others in quicksand. The flight of the hero with the dead man's savings, at a moment of radical change, may be a transposed inversion of Godbout's own departure from Quebec for Ethiopia in the mid-1950s, on the eve of the Quiet Revolution. (The author's Ethiopian experience, plus the famine that devastated that country in the 1980s, would be fused with a teaching stint at Berkeley to nourish *Une histoire américaine*(1986)/*An American Story*.)

In *Le Couteau sur la table* (1965)/*Knife on the Table*, Godbout, continuing his geographical and psychological odyssey, once again presents an anonymous narrator-hero who is obsessed with the problem of his identity. Past and present coexist in a state of uneasy tension as the hero, a former deserter from the Canadian army in the Prairies, returns to the West after ten years to resume a teen-age liaison with an anglophone, Patricia, daughter and heiress of a wealthy couple—an Irish woman and a Czech-born Jew. The narration, centred mainly on the first phase of the relationship, alternates between it and the one in the present, but the two often merge, sometimes within the same sentence. During the first phase, the young couple traverse Canada from west to east on their way to Montreal, with an accompaniment of place-names and railway stations that the narrator perceives as alien to him. Once in Montreal, the kept and subservient lover of the rich *étrangère*, he is caught between her and the sensitive Madeleine, a compatriot who had grown up amid the smokestacks of the east-end. The hero's hesitation in choosing between the two causes Madeleine to take her life, while carrying the narrator's child. He then flees to the US with some stolen drugs that he peddles, pursued by the police. After a stay in a Mexican village he returns to Western Canada to renew the decade-old liaison with Patricia. The wintry season of the relationship ends in the spring of 1963 when the first FLQ bombs explode in Quebec and the narrator contemplates (and commits?) the murder of his mistress. The theme of the search for national identity is clearly inscribed in the plot structure, with its 'philosophical' voyage across Canada, the US, and Mexico; the symbolic triangle formed by the narrator, Patricia, and Madeleine; and the intertwining of English and French in the characters' speech. The narrator frequently verbalizes his feelings of cultural alienation, and his pessimism over his socio-cultural position leads him to mock Quebec's motto (*Je me souviens*), which he adamantly negates (*Je ne veux plus me souvenir*). This same depression dominates his wanderings with his friends in Montreal's bars and main thoroughfares, 'named after the Anglo-Saxon governors who beat us down . . .', and his oversimplified ethnocentric evocations of the 1837 Rebellion. The narrator, in fact, presents the adversaries in the conflict of politico-cultural forces as two 'ethnic classes' (in Marcel Rioux's words), dividing them along the mythically stereotyped lines of the commercially minded, uncultured anglophones and the spiritually oriented, aesthetic francophones. In *Le Couteau sur la table*, then—a fascinatingly structured and sometimes poetic work—the stress is on differentiation (which Rioux links to periods of withdrawal and defensive nationalism) and on major characters who are more ethno-political symbols than real people.

In *Salut Galarneau!* (1967) / *Hail Galarneau!* Godbout's narrator-hero is no longer anonymous, and the quest for identity is concentrated within the geographical confines of Quebec itself—or, more precisely, on the pages of the novel François Galarneau is writing. The self-employed proprietor of a hotdog stand ('*Au roi du hot dog*') in the Montreal suburbs, François Galarneau is a former tavern waiter, construction worker, and clerk who quit secondary school because he found his classes irrelevant. He is not only a narrator-actor but also a narrator-writer whose frequently hilarious observations are set down in two school notebooks that become the novel itself, and contain some of Godbout's best satire. Galarneau's invention of the neologism '*vécrire*' (a fusion of '*vivre*', and '*écrire*'), as a goal towards which he strives, treats symbolically a major conflict that faces any writer. Otherwise the semi-educated Galarneau speaks a moderate form of *joual*. Some of the words he conceives of as English he puts into italics; but there are many others he does not recognize as bastardized and that naturally slip into his speech and writing.

The hotdog vendor suffers a broken marriage, then the loss of his mistress to his brother Jacques, an opportunistic professional writer. Following these setbacks he isolates himself from the world by building a concrete wall around his home (symbol of the traditional xenophobic, isolationist Quebec) and spends days being bombarded by television commercials. In the long run he decides to assume his true self and rejoin his people, to leave his walled barrier and offer his manuscript to the city and the world, including the *vendus* (sellouts) who have betrayed him. At the end he is reconciled with life: 'The sun ['Galarneau' in Quebec folklore] . . . warms our patch of ground . . . I fled away from it, but won't any longer.' The possessive adjective 'our' obviously has a significant collective (as well as individual) register.

Salut Galarneau! is a work of positive self-affirmation that parallels the growth of neo-nationalism during the year of Montreal's hosting of Expo 67 and General de Gaulle's cry, '*Vive le Québec libre!*' Godbout has himself explained its double purpose: 'I wanted it to give people a taste for life but without hiding reality'—the reality of cultural alienation. In comparison with the language of Godbout's two previous novels, the turn to popular French-Canadian speech from standard French is highly significant, and reflects a coming to terms with his 'differences' vis-à-vis both French and Anglo-American culture. Also, while there are still jibes at English-speaking Canadians, meaningful barbs are tossed, too, at Quebec politicians (including Premiers Lesage and Johnson), and the 'thieving' well-to-do of whatever origin. While there is a 'nationalist' note in the reconciliation with the *vendus* at the end of the novel, there is at the same time a stronger association with the common people and their speech, and greater recognition of class and political differentiation among the Québécois than was evident in the novelist's earlier works. Paralleling this is the novel's simpler, more direct form in comparison with the complex *nouveau roman* techniques of the two preceding novels. It is still, however, a highly original and imaginative work.

Hubert Aquin (1929-77), another novelist who emerged during the 1960s, is intimately related to the neo-nationalist *'texte national'*—a term coined by Jacques Godbout to describe novels that were mainly concerned with Quebec's place in Canada and the world—but in a more complex, contradictory, and tragic way. 'Aquin quickly became his own legend', as Fredric Jameson has put it, 'and sealed the mystery of his existence' by his suicide in March 1977 after a series of crises in his publishing and journalistic careers and a failed attempt to write another novel, *Obombre*, of which only fragments remain. Several books have been published on Aquin, and many studies continue to probe his work, especially his first novel, *Prochain épisode (1965, tr. 1967).

Several critics have analysed the intriguing contradictions of the title *Prochain épisode* (next instalment), which suggests a dramatic incident—possibly a revolutionary one—to erupt in the next episode of a serial publication. They have also seen in it an ironic recognition of the uncompleted novel-within-the novel that preoccupies the confined narrator of the work, and its parallel in Aquin's 'hero's' inability, within the novel to the second degree, to kill his quarry and re-unite with his beloved, both of which scenarios are projected to the *'prochain épisode'*. The source of this double failure is the inherent depression of an intellectual that is inextricably linked to the historical failures of the Québécois people to become independent.

The novel draws on aspects of Aquin's own life: his involvement in radical segments of the independence movement, his arrest in 1964 for illegal possession of a firearm after a self-publicized foray 'underground', his subsequent confinement to a psychiatric prison (where he wrote *Prochain épisode*—he was acquitted in 1965), and his travels through Switzerland. The double or mirror structure of *Prochain épisode* presents a narrator who is indeed under armed surveillance at a psychiatric institution while awaiting trial after an abysmal attempt at politically motivated violence. While there he attempts to write a novel in which his 'fictional' narrator, acting for an illegal movement closely resembling the FLQ, pursues, also unsuccessfully, the task of gunning down in Switzerland an RCMP agent. The latter has uncovered the movement's secret bank reserves in that country, thus threatening to deal it a powerful blow. The two main structures of the work constantly intertwine, finally fusing in the return of the narrator(s) to Canada, only to fall into a trap and imprisonment.

Like Godbout's heroes, Aquin's is also concerned with his identity, and in the novel-within-the novel the pursuer is totally confused by the three identities of his quarry—who claims at different times to be the 'historian' H. de Heutz, the 'banker' Carl von Ryndt, and the depressed 'Belgian' François-Marc Saugy. Hunter and hunted change roles several times in the picturesque Swiss landscape, but the 'fictional' hero constantly procrastinates before his assigned task. He is mesmerized by the luxurious castle where his target lives, and his resolution weakens as he gazes on its magnificent *objets d'art*, especially the symbolically charged bronze figure of two naked warriors in combat and Benjamin West's painting *The Death of General Wolfe*. Aquin in his essays stressed the attraction the colonizer's values and culture have for the colonized people, who suffer from an imposed 'amnesia' following their conquest and subsequently 'forget' their own individuality.

The triadic figure of the enemy's identity is also present in the three main figures of the 'fictional' plot—the narrator-hero, his lover, and the enemy—and the three narrative 'I's' of the work: the author-narrator, the author-narrator recalling his past whose lyrical effusions evoke various erotic-nationalist experiences and involvements, and the narrator-actor of the novel-within-the-novel. The triad is combined with dual tensions between the two main narrators and the protagonist and his enemy, as well as within the ambivalent female character designated only as 'K' (Quebec?), who appears to be at one and the same time the narrator's lover and fellow member of a secret FLQ-like cell *and* a double agent in cahoots with the RCMP 'banker'. It is strongly implied that it is she who tricks the narrator(s) into returning to Canada and falling prey to an ambush. There is also confusion between 'K' and the undesignated lover evoked in the lyrical-dream passages of the 'author-narrator'. These and other aspects of the novel-within-the-novel take on the parodic dimensions of a mock-epic with echoes of James Bond, the humour of which has hardly been noticed.

Prochain épisode is not only Aquin's first published novel but his most famous. Drawing upon his own tensions and his vision as a major representative of Quebec's neo-nationalism of the 1960s, he produced an outstanding, innovative, and complex work that transcends the concerns of the period.

Aquin published three novels in the 1960s. The first was followed by *Trou de mémoire* (1968) / *Blackout* (for which he refused a Governor General's Award on political grounds) and *L'Anti-phonaire* (1969) / *The Antiphonary*. His last published work during his lifetime was *Neige noire* (1974)/*Hamlet's Twin*.

Aquin's fiction became progressively more preoccupied with literary (rather than political) objectives in the works that followed *Prochain épisode*, until *Neige noire* where, as the author himself says, '*Le Québec est en creux*' (Quebec is at a low ebb) and there is hardly a discernible reference to mainstream political questions—although the final lesbian apotheosis of the work may be a strong feminist statement, as Patricia Smart has suggested. In *Trou de mémoire* the main character—the self-styled revolutionary and pharmacist Pierre-X. Magnant—undertakes the writing of a detective novel after raping, then murdering, his English-Canadian mistress, Joan Ruskin, in a ritualistic and symbolic act. He records his reflections, as well as his political views, in a *récit* that constitutes the bulk of the novel. Placed at the very beginning and near the end of this work are a letter to Magnant from of an African pharmacist and radical, Olympe, the lover of Joan's sister Rachel (a nurse in Abidjan), and Olympe's journal. While on a visit to Switzerland with Rachel, Olympe suffers the humiliation of his mistress's being raped by Magnant; he later commits suicide in Montreal. At the end of the novel Rachel is expecting Magnant's child, and after a long period of trauma plans to take on French-Canadian identity. Clearly the murder of Joan and rape of Rachel are reflections of the love-hate relationship already seen in *Prochain épisode* and represent a compensatory inversion of the historical process, with the Third World passages echoing 'colonized' Quebec. As Patricia Smart has written, Magnant's sexual and projected political violence is a reflection of his political and consequently erotic impotence. (Four years before this novel was published Michel van Schendel drew a parallel between the inability to love in the French-Canadian novel and the 'colonial' status of the Québécois.) Magnant specifically refers to Joan's inert body as a corpse and compares it to Canada, stressing that his violent act is a prelude to a host of others. The revolution Magnant dreams of is 'an immense, inaudible and original funereal cry uttered by a nation . . .' In *L'Antiphonaire* the explicit political matter is nearly invisible, except for a vague reference to the involvement of Robert Bernatchez, the heroine Dr Christine Forestier's lover, in a province-wide (but vaguely defined) political speaking tour. The series of rapes and other violent acts she endures, including those meted out by her epileptic husband (Aquin suffered from that disease), may point to the 'feminist' dénouement of *Neige noire* already referred to. In *L'Antiphonaire* the binary structure of the main plot is echoed by the (antiphonary) Renaissance material of Christine's doctoral thesis on epilepsy and becomes an authorial preoccupation. In *Neige noire*, Nicolas Vanasse's film-script for an adaptation of Shakespeare's masterwork, *Hamlet*, is intertwined with his technical/aesthetic commentaries and excruciatingly violent autobiographical confessions. Both these works stress questions of form, although brutality suffered by women is a recurring leitmotif.

Aquin's failed 'last book', as he himself described *Obombre*—fragments of which were published in *Liberté* in the issue of May-June 1981—completes the circle begun by *Prochain épisode*. The strange title, containing the word '*ombre*' (shadow), appears several times in the manuscript fragments and may portend the author's approaching death—which came within weeks of the writing of this handful of pages. The first syllable, 'ob', may suggest the prefix 'towards', or possibly the gulf of that name in the Arctic Ocean. The preoccupation with writing appears from the first lines, and again a binary geographical division is created—between Chicago, where the narrator is attempting to write a novel, and Utrecht, where he places the romantic action of his projected work. The 1837 Rebellion is evoked, as in *Prochain épisode*, with stress once more on its defeat. The Hamlet-like hesitation and deferring of action of the first novel reappears here, as the narrator declares that 'uncertainty [is] the prevalent modality of my incarnation', and expresses his intolerable suffering at 'surviving after having failed to write what one wanted to'—a masochistic regret that possibly contributed to Aquin's suicide. The epigraph to this sketchy piece—a quotation from the German philosopher Friedrich Schelling: 'The beginning becomes the beginning only at the end'—may be a key to the meaning of the title *Prochain épisode*.

The search for identity was also a major preoccupation of the young writers grouped around the journal *Parti pris* (1963-8), and its publishing house (1964-). Founded shortly after the first wave of FLQ bombings, *Parti pris* had both an *indépendantiste* and a Marxist orientation, advocating a sovereign and socialist Quebec. It was also strongly influenced by existentialism and by the anti-colonialist writings of Frantz Fanon, Jacques Berque, and Albert Memmi. The editors and contributors to *Parti pris* were mostly budding writers in their twenties, some (Paul Chamberland, Pierre Maheu) coming from educated middle-class backgrounds, while others (André Major, Jacques Renaud) were self-taught and of working-class origin. The journal occasionally published articles by Hubert Aquin, Jacques Godbout, and Jacques Ferron, who was a sort of father-figure for the *Parti pris* group. Novelists one generation older than they, like Claude Jasmin, also had books published by Les Editions Parti pris.

Although small and marginalized, *Parti pris* was instrumental in changing the self-image of the francophone majority of Quebec from that of *Canadiens français* to *Québécois*. In January 1965 a special issue, entitled '*Pour une littérature québécoise*', first proposed that new label, which rather quickly achieved universal acceptance and became the present consecrated term. That issue outlined the literary theories of the group, including the controversial call for the use of *joual*—the deformed, truncated, highly anglicized speech of the uneducated masses of Quebec, and especially Montreal—as a major literary tool. As Paul Chamberland wrote: 'One cannot render evil, putrefaction, disgust in a serene and correct tongue; my language must be shaken to its very foundations through the disfigurement inherent in our common speech, and in the lives of all of us.' The debate around *joual* writing raged for some years. Its partisans were given a boost by the immediate success of Michel Tremblay's *joual* masterpiece, *Les Belles-Soeurs* (1968), and by most of his subsequent plays. But some intellectuals who shared *Parti pris*'s political orientation condemned the literary use of *joual* as 'a disguised federalist plot' (Jean Marcel), while establishment figures like Justice Philippe Ferland declared it 'a symptom of the cancer eating away at our entire social organism, named Marxism', because it 'proclaims social levelling . . . and urges the people to take power . . .' While *joual* writing created an important corpus of works in the theatre and cinema, and provided an inspiration for some songwriters like Robert Charlebois, it has had a relatively short life-span in the novel genre, being perpetuated into the 1970s by only a few writers like Victor-Lévy Beaulieu and Tremblay himself. And this is how the *Parti pris* theoreticians originally saw it, for, as Gérald Godin wrote in the January 1965 issue, '*Joual* is our present, but international French our future.'

A short novel that epitomizes the *Parti pris* approach to literature is by **Jacques Renaud** (b. 1943): *Le Cassé* (1964)/*Broke City*, written when the author was just twenty-one. It is the best achievement of the *joual* writers of the period and the 'purest' work of its kind in its consistent use of the bruised dialect for both its narration *and* dialogue—a feature that distinguishes it from the social realism of Ringuet, Lemelin, and Roy. It is also the first French-Canadian novel to plumb the sub-culture of Montreal's lower depths. The plot is very simple. Tit-Jean, an unemployed youth with a reputation for violent fits of anger, is informed that his girlfriend, Philomène (Mémène), is being unfaithful to him and is frequenting a goofball-peddlar, Bouboule, whom Tit-Jean follows one night and kills. The temporary freedom he experiences after the murder gives way to a realization that he has solved nothing, and owns nothing: he is a *cassé*. The *joual* term of the title renders the idea of *broke*—but also *battered* or *beaten* in more normative French—and lends a symbolic dimension to the fate of the culturally and economically alienated main character. The narrative ends as it began with the word *cassé*.

Tit-Jean is isolated, with few social contacts except for his sexual ones with Mémène and casual links with one or two others of his milieu. His consciousness of time is defined by the day he receives his unemployment insurance. The rooms he lives in, near railway tracks, have rotting balconies, broken windows, and dirty sheets. His spiritual nourishment is restricted to the reading of the tabloid *Allô police*, and his speech is a non-language—a mixture of gallicized English, fragmented French, and curses and obscenities. His universe is not a homogeneous one, for there is social differentiation between the exploited—Tit-Jean and Mémène—and the exploiters, Bouboule and Berthe Larue, the wealthy lesbian student who pays Mémène for sexual favours.

Renaud broke with the realistic tradition of rendering popular speech solely in dialogue by eliminating the distinction between narration and direct discourse and having *joual* dominate both. The narrator is by no means a neutral observer, often fusing with his characters' consciousness and sometimes aggressively addressing the reader. He also uses the cinematic technique of 'cuts', without any authorial transitions, to create heightened drama and direct confrontation between reader and character. The narrator's comparison of the hero to 'a human bomb with a heart beating out a thick, red, nervous tick-tack...', as he waits for Bouboule to leave a restaurant, conjures up visions of the FLQ time-bombs set off only months before the book appeared. Renaud himself, in fact, belonged to a pre-FLQ underground group, the '*Réseau de résistance*' (Network of resistance).

Directly related to the political violence of the early 1960s is *Éthel et le terroriste* (1964)/*Ethel and the Terrorist* by **Claude Jasmin** (b. 1930). One of that prolific author's most successful works, it is a transposition of the incident in April 1963 when night-watchman William O'Neill (of French-Canadian descent) was killed by an FLQ bomb at a Montreal armoury. (In an earlier work, *La Corde au cou* (1961), Jasmin had anticipated socio-politically motivated violence in Quebec.) In *Éthel* the event is put back to February, and the locale of the explosion becomes a post-office.

Paul, who placed the bomb, flees to New York, according to his clandestine group's instructions, together with his mistress Éthel Rosensweig, whose family are survivors of the European Holocaust. During the couple's six-day stay in the metropolis, Paul searches his conscience to try to grasp why he committed the act and what its consequences will be. Fearful that Paul's liaison with a Jewish woman will hurt the nationalist cause, his movement orders him to break the relationship, but he refuses. He is 'tested' again by being obliged to take part in another violent incident at the Canadian consulate in New York. Éthel, who had lost many relatives in Europe during the Second World War, prods the conscience of her lover and influences him towards pacifism. Although she threatens to leave him over the death of the night-watchman, she is faithful to the end and returns with him to Montreal when he is summoned. Paul's fear and Éthel's constant preoccupation with possible victims of violence are relieved by escapist dreams and love-making. (Eroticism is another *constante* of the novels of the 1960s, when passion erupted, along with violence.) This very escapism lends a poetic dimension to the novel when Paul takes off on fanciful lyrical effusions.

As in other Jasmin novels, the hero is in flight and death hangs over his head. And Paul is a typical Jasmin hero: he comes from a poor background in a large working-class family of the Jarry Park area where the author himself grew up; he is imaginative, a semi-intellectual with an interest in music and drama; and he is filled with hatred for the ruling élites of his society and various kinds of *poseurs*. His contradictions and psychological characteristics parallel those of the (generally) young men who were involved in political violence in the FLQ and like movements of the 1960s. Éthel is less believable; her motivations for supporting Paul's political ideas and associations are never clearly established.

Jasmin's best novels are *Éthel et le terroriste* and *La Sablière* (1979)/*Mario*. Narrated by Clovis, an imaginative sixteen-year-old, *La Sablière* is a sometimes moving story about his younger autistic brother, Mario, whose stammer he cures by playacting. Mario is sent to an orphanage, from which Clovis assists his escape (after Mario has set fire to it) and the two hide out in a sand quarry in the Laurentian countryside until a Cistercian monk invites Mario to live and work on the Order's communal farm. The novel combines pathos and poetry.

Jacques Ferron's wedding of social and nationalist preoccupations linked him ideologically to the radical young authors around *Parti pris*, although his approach to literature and to traditional Quebec society was different from theirs. Essentially a *conteur*, a teller of tales, Ferron (1921-85) described himself as the last storyteller in the oral tradition and the first in the written tradition. He used archaic and folksy turns of phrase but shunned *joual*, except for the occasional word, which he assimilated into the phonetic system of Canadian French (*un clergimane*, *le gagnstère*). While the novelists and short-story writers of *Parti pris* were strong proponents of literary realism, Ferron combined socially committed themes with fantasy, myths, and legends. Also, while ferociously anti-clerical in most of his copious writings, he also had a certain feeling of warmth for the clergy, whom he saw as having played a positive role in giving coherence to the French-Canadian nationality during its centuries-long struggle for physical and cultural survival. He accords greater weight and value to the small community as against the larger, and in many of his fictional writings there is a constant tension between the south-shore municipalities of Longueuil and Ville Jacques-Cartier, where Ferron lived and practised medicine for years, and the metropolis, Montreal, on the other side of the St Lawrence, in a sort of Manichean dichotomy between good and evil. While the writers around *Parti pris* basically sought a clean break with the *agriculturiste* past of Quebec, Ferron always stressed the need to revive the constant exchange between town and countryside that had been lost, according to him, by massive industrialization and urbanization.

Ferron began his writing career as a brilliant producer of tales—his classic *Contes du pays incertain* was published in 1962—and critics consider him basically a *conteur* in the works he has designated as novels and in his plays. The phrase he coined, *le pays incertain*, became widely quoted and assimilated by Québécois intellectuals in search of a new definition for their socio-historical entity. As Ferron put it, 'The country seemed uncertain to me, and I had the following idea: I had to ensure its continued existence and then not think any more about it; then write in peace without worrying about my country, as is done in normal countries.' He also referred to Quebec as 'an incomplete country which would have liked to become sovereign . . .' The word 'sovereign', in this quote from 1969, has a very contemporary ring in 1991, as does Ferron's conclusion to the appendix to his *Confitures de coings* (1972): 'We must act quickly, the bridges have been burned behind us, there is no longer any salvation except through the complete occupation of the land.'

The plot of his first longer fiction work, *Cotnoir* (1962) / *Dr. Cotnoir*, is simple, even though the arrangement of its various threads is quite complex. The narrator is an unnamed young colleague and disciple of Cotnoir who attempts to grasp the meaning of the events that occurred ten years earlier and to communicate it to the reader, focusing on Cotnoir, whom he admires. He completely overturns chronological time through a circular account that begins and ends with Cotnoir's funeral, and the order of which is regulated by the impact of certain key events on him. The resulting 'time montage' (Jean Marcel) is constructed not only between chapters but also between sentences and words. It is left to readers to reassemble the chronological sequence. The action is set in the south-shore working-class suburb of Ville Jacques-Cartier, and in the nearby middle-class area of Longueuil where Dr Cotnoir, who serves the former, lives. Emmanuel, around thirty, has lost his longtime job as a chicken-plucker after the death of his employer. He wanders from tavern to tavern, ending up in Bordeaux Jail ('crazy section') after urinating from a balcony on passersby. Aubertin, a coal-delivery man, who had not seen his cousin Emmanuel for years, is summoned by a social worker in Montreal and asked to take his 'cured' relative home for a transitional period of two weeks. At the Aubertin home in Ville Jacques-Cartier, Emmanuel misbehaves repeatedly until Mme Aubertin has to call in the family physician, Cotnoir. The compassionate doctor—ever sympathetic to those of the working-class—makes little of the 'crisis', advising that Emmanuel be placed on the train for Quebec City with a view to getting a job at a nearby lumber camp. That very evening M. Aubertin, Cotnoir, and the narrator take Emmanuel to the railway station, where he breaks away from them and disappears, asserting his independence, and takes the train to Quebec himself. Dr Cotnoir dies the next morning, mumbling about 'a ticket for Quebec'. Emmanuel, however, thrives and we meet him ten years later at a wedding at the Aubertins. Clearly the doctor's advice was his salvation.

Ferron has indicated that models for the two main characters, Cotnoir and Emmanuel, were found in real life. Evidently a Dr Cotnoir preceded him in his medical practice in the Gaspé in the late 1940s. But the fictional doctor is obviously a composite of that practitioner and Ferron himself. He once revealed that the writing of *Cotnoir* was for him a cathartic personal experience: 'I knew Emmanuel. I didn't dare put him on the Quebec City train. He died in Bordeaux, I think.'

Cotnoir is the first of a number of books in which Ferron probes 'deviant' mental behaviour in works obviously related to his experience as a physician at the Montreal mental hospital, Saint-Jean-de-Dieu. Others are *L'Amélanchier* (1970)/*The Juneberry Tree*—in which the fantasy of a childhood garden merges with the effort of the narrator, Tinamer, and her jailer-father, to save an emotionally deprived young prisoner—and *Les Roses sauvages* (1971)/*Wild Roses*, where mental breakdown and suicide are probed, as is strident English unilingualism in Moncton.

Les Confitures de coings (1972) / *Quince Jam* is a revised version of Ferron's novel *La Nuit* (1965): in between the two publication years there occurred the October Crisis of 1970. The author again weds realistic, autobiographical elements with fantasy and personal myth-making, constructing a novel that is partly an act of redemption for having betrayed his ideals in 1949, shortly after he had become a Communist and was arrested during an anti-NATO demonstration in Montreal. Ferron, who belonged to every left-wing party in Quebec over a period of several decades, had been converted to communism 'by illumination, without reading the sacred texts', while recuperating from tuberculosis in the Laurentians. During his trial, in order to be acquitted he accepted a sympathetic judge's suggestion that his prostrate position when he was arrested was caused by inebriation rather than by actual manhandling by police. Thus he lost his soul, and *Confitures* metaphorically recounts his retrieval of it.

François Ménard is an accountant at the head-office of the Majestic Bank in the usual south-shore locale—a conformist suburbanite who hopes one day to be named a branch manager. In what may be a dream, he is awakened one night by a phone call from Frank Campbell, a recurring Ferron character (he is called Frank Anacharsis Scot in *Le Ciel de Québec* (1969)/*The Penniless Redeemer*), who is clearly based on Frank Scott, the late poet, McGill law professor, and translator of Anne Hébert's verse. Ferron had a long friendship with Scott that ended abruptly following Scott's support of the War Measures Act in 1970. Ferron's heroes have an obsessive love-hate relationship with the fictional representation of Scott, and one could trace the novelist's ideological evolution through the changing contours of this 'imaginary' character. His relative benign traits in *La Nuit*, for example, fell by the wayside in the revised *Confitures*. Here Campbell is described as a police agent and forensic expert who invites Ménard to meet him at the Montreal morgue. Their rendezvous brings back repressed memories of the accountant's past—which replicate Ferron's arrest in 1949. Over a night of initiatory incidents, including a sexual encounter with a black prostitute who reminds him of his habit-clad mother when she studied at the Ursuline convent, he returns to a bar to find Campbell dead, slumped over his favourite quince jam, which Ménard had given him as a (poisoned) 'present'. After this cathartic event he cheerfully returns by taxi to his suburban home, having pocketed Frank Campbell's notebook, wherein he finds details of the latter's years of secret surveillance and plans to assimilate François and all French Canadians. Ménard arrives home before his wife wakes, finds her habitual passivity gone, shaves, and goes off to work as usual, bathed in glorious sunshine. He has retrieved his soul and his commitment to his people.

Frank and François are linked by the commonality of their names, their birth in Louiseville (Scott was in fact born in Quebec City), and their twenty-year-old association, dating from the police beating of François in which Frank took part. Frank is 'the representative of the Rhodesians of Montreal' (a phrase coined by René Lévesque), the supposed 'liberals' who betrayed the Québécois in their hour of need in the October Crisis (when the FLQ requested that Ferron act as intermediary between them and the government). In the rather angry appendix to *Confitures*, in which he attacks Scott, Ferron also flays Hugh MacLennan, another supporter of the War Measures Act, telling us that he considered *La Nuit* a sequel (*'une suite'*) to *Two Solitudes*.

Although Ferron is always very sensitive to the toiling humanity of the south-shore communities—where, in fact, both francophone *and* anglophone workers live—in *Confitures* he exhibits an ideological stance centred on an ethnic determinism that sees the francophones of Quebec as a dominated ethnic class, and the anglophones, taken as a whole, as the dominators. Thus the nationalist side of Ferron eventually overtook his deep consciousness of social class. This is seen in *Le Saint-Élias* (1972) *[The Saint Elias*, a historical novel covering nearly a hundred years, 1850 to 1940. The title is the name of a ship (after that of a local priest), launched in 1896. It is also a metaphor. Under its captain, Pierre Maheu (named for the editor of *Parti pris*), it breaks out of the confines of the Gulf of St Lawrence (escaping the village and Quebec itself) to sail into the Atlantic southward, its sails stretched out to the wide world—though it returns. The novel is also about a family dynasty founded by a Métis, Marguerite, and her husband Philippe Cossette (named for the provincial Créditiste leader of the time), who is the owner of the ship and the richest man in the region. The family chronicle suggests the bringing together of politically differentiated strains of Quebec francophone society, so that its collective memory can be preserved, its heritage perpetuated, and the social spectrum of Quebec life unified. *Le Saint-Élias* has therefore been called 'a novel of reconciliation'.

There is no question that Jacques Ferron is one of the most original and imaginative authors Quebec has produced, exhibiting in his best works a mastery of expression, humour, pathos, make-believe, and a well of warmth for common folk. But it is also true that sometimes, as Gilles Marcotte has said, his work suffers from excessive prattle and uncreative hermeticism. Ferron himself has acknowledged that his obsession with the 'uncertain country' forced him to mix into the beautiful work he dreamed of 'a dose of rhetoric and more or less camouflaged political discussion, all of this rather badly stirred together, with ambiguity, confusion and even rambling.'

Marie-Claire Blais (b. 1939) came into immediate prominence (or notoriety) with her first novel, *La Belle Bête* (1959) / *Mad Shadows*, published when she was not yet twenty. With its vaguely sketched, grim rural landscape, scenes of physical and moral ugliness, disfigurement, pyromania, murder and suicide, it shocked the most traditional (clerical) critics, while impressing all who were open to the new. With more than thirty years of creativity behind her and some forty works of fiction, poetry, and drama— the best-known of which include the first volume in a semi-autobiographical trilogy, *Les Manuscrits de Pauline Archange* (1968)/*The Manuscripts of Pauline Archangel* (containing all three novels in translation), which traces the emergence of a writer against all the odds of heredity and environment—the *Wunderkind* of Québécois letters continues to publish regularly, although not always on the same high level of achievement. Here I shall discuss particularly the masterful *Une saison dans la vie d'Emmanuel* (1965)/*A Season in the Life of Emmanuel* and another prize-winning novel published twenty years after her first, *Le Sourd dans la ville* (1979) / *Deaf to the City*, to give an idea of her range.

Une saison is set in a sketchily defined rural setting at a generally unspecified time, although the presence of '*le fleuve*' (a river emptying into the sea) and shoe factories, and the evoking of 'the war' suggest the author's native Quebec City area in the early 1940s. The Emmanuel of the title is a baby born on the very day the story begins, into a crowded, dishevelled, abjectly poor household where his father and mother are referred to only as '*l'homme*' and '*la mère*'. In a nearly anonymous amalgam, children are often referred to by number ('*Le Septième*' is one of the important characters, while Emmanuel is '*Le Seizième*') or by letter ('*les grandes A*', '*les petites A*'). Even Grand-Mère Antoinette—the devout, conservative, massive *magna mater* of the shambles of a family—confuses the categories of family members: 'There they all were, the grandchildren, the children, the nieces and nephews; you thought they were buried in the snow . . . or dead for years, but they're always there . . .' Her grandson Jean-Le Maigre, however, she does not confuse. He is her favourite. He writes poems and journals and projects in his writing a different kind of world than the cultural wasteland he grew up in. Jean's 'autobiography' is integrated into the story as it is read by Antoinette. She saves it from being destroyed by his brutal father, who wants to use the manuscripts as toilet paper.

Before Le Septième and his brother Pomme leave for a shoe factory in the city, Antoinette exclaims: 'O heaven . . . take pity on these animals being led to the slaughter . . .' Le Septième writes to her longingly, asking for news of home—'And the cow Clementine, Grandma/ And the little calf, Grandma/ With or without spots/ And the pig Marthuroulou what colour/ Grandma.' Blais smoothly interweaves such tender passages with scenes of lust, as when the boorish notary Larouche, a client of Héloise in the brothel she has been working in since she left the convent, is accused of 'trampling her youth, without regard for the misery of her body', just as her father nightly rapes her bewildered, shadowy, delirious mother.

The 'season' of the title is the winter, or the end of it, and the novel concludes with the coming of warmer, sunnier days, as the baby claps and Antoinette predicts better things to come, although the touching poet, Jean-Le Maigre, has died of consumption; Héloïse continues working in a brothel; and Pomme loses three fingers in a shoe-factory machine.

This resumé, however, does not give an adequate picture of the novel's thrust for, while parodying the traditional family celebrated by rural myth and undermining its pillars, the Church and the family, the novel revived a *carnavalesque* and grotesque register that was rare in the Quebec novel.

Stress on the novel's naturalistic traits and socio-historical significance by critics has now given way to emphasizing its fanciful, mock-realistic style, as when 'a camera eye' in the novel's opening focuses on Antoinette's large feet, seen from the 'viewpoint' of the baby Emmanuel. If the setting can be compared to Laberge's *La Scouine*, the mode borrows more from Girard's *Marie Calumet* in its *rabaissement* (lowering) of authority figures—particularly in the satirical system of naming (Théodule Crapula, the sadistic monk; Mlle Lorgnette, the teacher) and goes far beyond it in its stress on bodily functions—mastication, elimination, copulation, masturbation, etc.

There is a 'series of perspectival views' in *Une saison*, 'behind each of which stands the ironic presence of an anonymous narrator . . . .' (Rosmarin Heidenreich). In *La Sourd dans la ville* there is also a third-person narratorial presence that organizes the story material, but one bereft of the irony and judgements of the earlier novel. This presence is thus more 'objective' (except for the occasional vague *nous* and *on*) but is equally omniscient, since it enters the consciousness of the various major and even minor characters. The entire novel is in fact a single uninterrupted paragraph that covers, in terms of conceptual time, the action of a few hours on an unidentified Friday. Shifts from one consciousness to another are made with conjunctions (*mais*, *et*). 'There is almost no dialogue, just a prolonged, anguished contemplation described in lengthy twining sentences that shift from character to character, from present to past, often within a phrase' (Joyce Marshall). Both experimental and yet in its narrative thrust conventional, this novel has the power to carry the reader along without a pause.

While there are some similarities in narrative techniques between *Une saison* and *Le Sourd dans la ville*, an atmosphere of doom hangs over the latter (unrelieved by the *carnavalesque* humour and exuberance of the former), which reflects philosophical and ethical considerations concerning human suffering, death, war, and fascism that are evident in Blais's writing of the last fifteen years or so. The literal meaning of the French title, 'the deaf one in the city', refers to Death, which hovers over Mike, the cancerous child of Gloria, the proprietor of the rundown Hôtel des Voyageurs where the action is centred, and over Florence, the wealthy woman who takes shelter there by chance after her husband deserts her and whose 'fatal act' of eventual suicide 'was already imprinted on her'. The image of the title appears towards the end of the novel when Florence, contemplating Mike, thinks: '. . . death stood there, it was nothing more than a deaf presence in the city . . . .'

The sordid environment is bathed in crime (Mike's father had been gunned down in front of the hotel; his sister Lucia is a child prostitute; his mother's lover, Charlie, is in prison) but is tempered by the luminous presence of a sometime passerby, Judith Langenais (better known as Lange, 'angel'), a junior college philosophy teacher and sometime lover of Florence. (The theme of lesbianism emerged openly in Blais's work in the late 1970s in *Les Nuits de l'Underground* (1978) / *Nights in the Underground*, after some texts dealing with male homosexuality, and is again central in her 1989 novel *L'Ange de la solitude*.) Feminism is touched on in Florence's reflections on her husband ('he thought I belonged to him, but it was a lie') and on males in general ('her inner existence . . . would have perhaps been peaceful if she had not known men'). But she can't get the memory of her husband out of her head and constantly evokes his sandals, which remind her of Christ. The paintings of the Norwegian expressionist Edvard Munch (*The Madonna*, *Three Girls on a Bridge* . . . but also *Pain*, *The Sick Child* and *The Scream*), which Florence recalls having seen in art galleries or owned as reproductions that hung in her apartment, bring both solace and suffering. (Mireille Dansereau's 1987 film adaptation seized upon the highly visual quality of the narration, and used *The Scream* to establish a parallel between its frightening child and the dying Mike.)

The presence of Death, in the title and its variations, and in the thoughts and final suicidal act of Florence, is not only centred on the individual but also has a collective component. Judith Lange speaks to her students about the lesser-known Nazi death camps of Mauthausen and Terezin, which she calls 'monuments to cruelty', where people were destroyed 'voluptuously'. She tells them that 'indifference . . . is the passion of Terror'. Because she shares these thoughts with Florence, the older woman reflects on her physicist son, he 'who had never talked to her about the murders of History . . . perhaps because he was born to commit others.' This leads her to the thought that science was 'the Great Terror of which the future might be made.' Florence also recalls seeing on TV 'a man about to be hanged because he refused to go to war . . . but it was only a movie.'

The term *carnavalesque* has also been applied to **Roch Carrier** (b. 1937), and especially to his best-known novel **La Guerre, yes sir!* (1968). He is one of the most popular Québécois writers in English Canada, thanks to the translations of many of his novels. The two books that form a trilogy with *La Guerre—Floralie, où es-tu?* (1969)/*Floralie, Where Are You?*, and *Il est par là le soleil* (1970)/*Is It the Sun, Philibert?*—and several others are inspired by his childhood and youth in a small village of the Beauce region south of Quebec City where he was born and grew up. The trilogy is centred on the Corriveau family and their young neighbour, Philibert, who takes part in a funeral wake at the Corriveau home with his father, the brutish butcher/gravedigger, Arsène, in the first novel, and later flees his home town for adventure in Montreal, where he dies in a car accident, in the third. Between the two poles is the nightmarish wedding-night of Anthyme and Floralie Corriveau, some thirty years before their son returns in a coffin from Britain. Carrier shows nostalgia for the close relationships of a tightly knit community and at the same time a consciousness of its pettiness, ignorance, and isolation. Like other writers who became prominent in the 1960s, Carrier has been attracted by nationalism, which sometimes takes on rather stereotyped forms in his writing.

In *La Guerre* the action is in fact concentrated in an off-the-beaten-track Quebec village on a single winter day during the Second World War. Six anglophone soldiers wade through the snow from the tiny railway station with the casket of Corriveau, a village soldier who had died ludicrously in Britain when he stepped on a land-mine outside a latrine. In the village hides a deserter and one man who cut off his hand to avoid gong to war. Another local soldier, Bérubé, arrives there on leave with his bride, the ex-prostitute Molly from Newfoundland. During the wake that makes up most of the action there is a raucous and earthy orgy of eating and drinking that ends in a brawl between the 'French-Canadian swine' and the stereotyped ramrod English-speaking soldiers. The deserter, fearing arrest, shoots and kills one of the soldiers, evening the 'score' at one dead each in '*la petite guerre*' that is most palpable to the village folk. This localized war is reflected in the hybridly bilingual title and by the ironic coupling of Bérubé and Molly. Bérubé's main task in the army was cleaning outhouses in Gander (one of many scatological references), together with other 'lesser breeds': Poles, Italians, Hungarians, and Greeks. Though ensconced in the dead soldier Corriveau's bed with Molly, Bérubé returns to the wake to pick a fight with Arsène, whom he had heard making light of a soldier's life. During the ensuing fight between the villagers and the soldiers Bérubé is tempted to defend his fellow francophones but, confused as to his identity, follows the orders of the sergeant to expel the troublemakers. Frustrated by his own powerlessness and that of the villagers, he redirects his violence on his own folk. These scenes are among the most convincing of the novel, the genre of which has been described as 'caricatural realism'.

André Belleau has pointed to several major elements of the *carnavalesque* in *La Guerre*, based on the coexisting opposition between the serious and the comic: the contrast between the guzzling irreverent villagers and the impassive anglophone soldiers who stand stiffly at attention through most of the wake; Arsène, beaten nearly to a pulp by Bérubé, laughs with the onlookers; the British flag that covered Corriveau's casket serves as a table-cloth during the gluttony; the pig slaughtered by Arsène for the wake is compared by his son to Christ on the cross. One could add the 'grotesque realism' of the game of hockey played by the village children with Joseph's severed hand serving as a puck. While hilarious in its truculence and poignant in its portrayal of Bérubé, Carrier's use of the *carnavalesque* still relies too heavily on caricature, and in his attempt to bury forever the pastoral tradition he creates a village of brutes and ignoramuses, almost without exception. (Could this be one of the reasons for the novel's great success in English Canada, as for that of the stage adaptation performed at Ontario's Stratford Festival?) It is much more unidimensional in this regard than *Une saison dans la vie d'Emmanuel*, lacking the profuse tenderness that is such an important ingredient of Blais's work.

Similarly reductive in its nationalism is Carrier's *Il n'y a pas de pays sans grand-père* (1977)/*No Country Without Grandfathers*, which, despite some fine descriptive evocations of the life of Vieux-Thomas, most artificially builds the plot around Queen Elizabeth's visit to Quebec in 1964 and the resulting riot, which is fictionalized through the arrest and imprisonment of the hero's grandson. The work, kindly called an 'essay-novel' (Gilles Dorion), has been better described as 'more of a statement of Carrier's ideological and literary affiliations than an original story' (Sherry Simon), the latter links being with the Manichean lineage of *Maria Chapdelaine*, Groulx's *L'Appel de la race*, and Savard's *Menaud, maître-draveur*. The butcher Arsène and Anthyme Corriveau of *La Guerre* appear in episodic reminiscences in this novel, which, in idealistic fashion, reproduces Quebec's traditional attitudes to agriculture, the Church, and women.

A more ambivalent attitude to nationalism is seen in the work of that other *Wunderkind* of Quebec letters, **Réjean Ducharme** (b. 1942), who, meteor-like, pierced the literary landscape in the sixties with his verbal fireworks, highly imaginative plot structures, and bizarre characters. There is both a sharing of nationalist feelings by some characters and a rejection of certain manifestations of nationalism by others.

The major theme of Ducharme's work is the refusal of adulthood by his child-heroes, or the attempt by his older heroes to cling to the fabulous and free contours of their early years. In his brilliant first published novel, *L'Avalée des avalés* (1966)/*The Swallower Swallowed*, the central character is the narrator, Bérénice Einberg, the daughter of quarrelling Polish immigrants—a Catholic mother and a Jewish father. It is in the form of a journal, with undated brief entries that cover six years in Bérénice's life, from age nine to fifteen. Her family lives in an old abbey on an island in the St Lawrence near Montreal. Bérénice is torn between her love for her brother Christian and her love-hate relationship with her mother. She soon becomes callous towards everyone but her brother, choosing to 'swallow' everything she encounters rather than be swallowed herself. Her life thereupon unfolds in pain and farce.

Because of her affection for Christian, she is exiled to New York by her father to a Jewish relative. Before she leaves, though, she kills one of her mother's favourite cats in an act of transposed matricide. In New York she studies languages and dance, and develops a close friendship with Constance Chlore (chlorine), who later dies in an accident. She writes hundreds of love-letters to Christian, but he is indifferent to her feelings.

When she flees her uncle Zio's home and reaches the Canadian border, she writes in her journal: 'Once there, without a better country than mine and a better destination than the abbey, I decide to retreat.' She eventually does return home, but is again sent away by her father, this time to Israel, during its war of independence, where she exults: 'This country is my country . . . I thought I belonged nowhere . . . Here I feel I have roots.' But this feeling does not last long either for, repelled by hyper-nationalism, she again declares herself 'stateless'. In Israel, too, there is tragedy, for Bérénice uses her lesbian suitor, Gloria, as a shield against Syrian gunfire, thus causing the young woman's death.

Bérénice rejects the adult world ('One must avoid adults as one does quicksand'), as do other heroes and heroines of Ducharme. She creates her own anti-social language, '*le bérénicien*', in which, as she says, 'the verb *to be* is never conjugated without the verb *to have*', suggesting a socio-political interpretation as well as an ontological one. While in New York she is attracted to one Jerry de Vignac, to whom she proposes a hotel escapade: '. . . there we will not make love but tenderness; we'll make tenderness there until we are emptied, dried out, freed, dead. A little tenderness, and death . . . . That's all.' This evasion of sexuality, a constant feature of Ducharme's prose, has been commented on *ad infinitum*. It can be seen both as an attempt to maintain childhood purity or as a reflection of the puritanism of traditional French-Canadian upbringing, or perhaps as a dialectical combination of both.

The attraction between sisters and brothers, the main form of the rejection of adult sexuality, recurs in all of Ducharme's prose works. In *L'Hiver de force* (1973)/*Wild to Mild* Nicole and André Ferron sleep in the same bed but do not engage in sexual congress, or in petting. (The model for these recurring couples is starfish, described in *La Fille de Christophe Colomb* (1969) as 'sleeping one next to the other/Without being dirty pigs.') They are clearly brother and sister, but the narrator surrounds them with a certain degree of ambiguity, which has caused some critics to wonder whether in fact they are man and wife. They live in a run-down apartment in the Plateau Mont-Royal area of Montreal and decide to denounce everything—good books and films, whether read and seen or not, 'hippies, artists, journalists, Taoists, nudists', and all those who wish to co-opt them to their causes, 'until the next new wave'. Thanks to their friends, the painter Laïnou and the film star/director, Catherine (also known as 'la Toune' and 'Petit Pois'), they mingle with various artistic élites. Catherine is married to publisher/writer Roger Degrandpré, a leading light in the Parti Québécois. Nicole and André live vicariously through Catherine's stardom and fame, and worship her until their failed idyll at her parents' summer cottage, where they reject her attempts to sully them through drugs—then find that she has rejected them once and for all. Against their will—since the result of their general disillusionment, both with conventional and 'avant-garde' society, is to do nothing—they see themselves forced at the end of the novel to become proof-readers for the PQ and thus enter, in the middle of summer, '*l'hiver de force*'—the metaphoric straitjacket of winter. Against the artificiality of the oppressive commercial, mechanical, and technological environment, they take solace in their sacramental bedside book and travelling companion *La Flore laurentienne* (1935) by Brother Marie-Victorin, an illustrated compendium of Quebec's plants.

Ducharme's novels are not without a nationalist thrust. In *Le Nez qui voque* (1967) the narrator Mille Milles (thousand miles) makes reference to the origin of the name Canada, 'in the Spanish words *aca* and *nada* which mean: nothing here'; reacts angrily against the immigrant restaurateurs for whom he works ('the Greeks and Romans...') when they refuse to speak to him in French; draws attention to his ugliness and sums up his feelings of non-belonging thus: 'Poor Mille Milles who, in addition to being all dirty, is a French Canadian.' In the 'novel' in rhymed quatrains, *La Fille de Christophe Colomb*, the irony is evident in this allusion to the heroine's dog Cabot: 'Colombe taught Cabot her language/He's bilingual: he barks and speaks. How beautiful!' In *L'Hiver de force* the narrator, André Ferron, and Nicole, working as proof-readers, take pride in giving the public 'copy in real, correct French', amidst the flood of Americanized commercial products and ridiculous bilingual signs: *'Now Playing Aujourdhui* et *Coming Soon Bientôt.* C'est beau.' In this same work, however, André lashes out at hypocritical 'radical' *indépendantistes* who live in the chic area of Outremont and exploit his and Nicole's affections and labour. Finally, in *Les Enfantômes* (1976)—the title fusing 'enfants' and 'fantôme', as *Le Nez qui voque* is a wordplay on 'nose' and 'equivocal' (*l'équivoque*)—the narrator, Vincent Falardeau, is (unhappily) married to an anglophone from Arnprior, Ontario, named Alberta Turnstiff(!), but is drawn constantly to his sister Fériée (a phonic wordplay on 'free' and 'fairy-like') in a triangle that, in addition to Ducharme's habitual incestuous pulls, has ethno-political overtones.

Ducharme's much-praised inventiveness with words is surely one of his most characteristic and original features. This is summed up by Asie Azothe, friend and fellow-traveller of the narrator of *L'Océantume* (1968)—another neologism based on the word *'l'amertume'* (bitterness), but which also contains *'la mer'* (the sea)—thus: 'All that counts is what you invent, what you create.' Mille Milles in *Le Nez* declares himself a poet, 'not a vulgar prose-writer'. We have already seen how Ducharme's fertile imagination functions in terms of titles, characters' names, and puns. One quickly becomes aware that he has read the symbolist and surrealist poets and that his 'derision shakes conventional language, consecrated ideas, society, culture' (Jean Marmier). As Gilles Dorion has said, these plays on words are captivating, then annoying, 'unless one has a particularly strong sense of humour and one accepts that the novelist hides behind this rhetoric to camouflage his existential anguish.'

The meaning of Ducharme's novels is elusive. One reason for this is that he constantly contradicts himself, as we have seen regarding his treatment of Quebec nationalism. Michel van Schendel wrote of *L'Avalée* that the reader is constantly 'wedged into a system of rejection and acceptance, of successive identities which are resolved by their elimination.' But he also pointed out that

Ducharme alone could not 'make coherent the new values' that were emerging from the old. Perhaps there is a key here to the paradoxical nature of Ducharme's writing in a period of *anomie*, when an outdated normative system had not yet been fully replaced by an alternative one.

NOVELISTS WRITING OUTSIDE THE 'TEXTE NATIONAL'

Other novelists—including Gabrielle Roy and Yves Thériault, who were well established—wrote important and striking works of fiction in the 1960s that were somewhat marginal to the *texte national*.

  Gabrielle Roy's *La Montagne secrète* (1961)/*The Hidden Mountain* is the story of a self-taught painter, Pierre Cadorai, based to some extent on the author's friend René Richard, who guided her on a tour of the Ungava Peninsula in the summer of 1961. The first part is set in the Northwest Territories (and, briefly, northern Manitoba), where Pierre meets a gold prospector and other fleeting persons whom he sketches, including the waitress Nina ('. . . he wanted to capture her features, which was his way of defending human beings') and the trapper Steve Sigurdsen. The second part finds Pierre in Ungava, where he discovers a fabulous mountain at sunset, an image that will remain with him for the rest of his life and that he will try vainly to reproduce on canvas. He meets the missionary Father Le Bonniec, who expresses a central thought of Roy's: 'To create . . . doesn't that mean to protest with one's entire soul?' In the final part of the novel Pierre is in Paris, where he studies painting but vegetates and finally succumbs to terminal illness. Before he dies he paints his own self-portrait (Roy died before the first volume of her autobiography was published), and in a vision finally recaptures in his imagination the magnificent mountain that he had named '*la Resplendissante*' (the Radiant One). But he is able to reproduce it only in fragmented form in touches of mauve (interpreted by André Brochu as representing at one and the same time the heart of the mountain and a loving human heart) before pain pierces his chest and immobilizes his hand. His dream of encapsulating 'in a single canvas . . . the entire object, the entire subject; everything that he was: all his experience, all his love, and thus attain infinite hope . . .' was never to be realized. A final thought crosses Pierre's mind: 'What dies, unexpressed, with a life, seemed to him the only death.'

La Montagne secrète offers insight into Roy's 'aesthetics of narrative' (André Brochu), and Ellen R. Babby points particularly to the use in the centre of the novel of *Hamlet*, which Pierre struggles to read, finding in it a 'spark' of profound meaning. Babby relates Pierre's discovery to a 'concern with language and identity . . . shared by the majority of Roy's characters', who ardently 'desire to communicate [through verbal and non-verbal codes], to be heard and recognized . . . .' She sees a self-reflexive expression of Roy's creative aim in Hamlet's words: 'If thou didst ever hold me in thy heart,/Absent thee from felicity awhile,/And in this harsh world draw thy breath in pain / To tell my story.'

La Rivière sans repos (1970) contains the novel-length title story—published in English as *Windflower* (1970)—and three shorter stories. In what may be an allegorical setting in the Far North, in the region of Fort Chimo, Roy probes some of her important concerns: cultures in contact and in conflict, primitive carefreeness and civilization, the search for identity. Elsa Kumachuk, an Inuit, is torn between her attraction to white ways and the pull of her own heritage after she is raped by an American soldier and left to bear a blond, blue-eyed son she names Jimmy. As the boy begins to grow, she moves north with her Uncle Ian, who lives according to the old ways, so that Jimmy will not have to enter the white school system. But in time they return to Fort Chimo and she re-enters the white world, making souvenirs on a sewing-machine. After Jimmy's persistent questions about his father go unanswered, he finally flees to the US and eventually becomes a bomber-pilot in Viet Nam. When that war is over she is left with nothing but what her neighbours tell her of the radio messages they heard when he flew over Fort Chimo.

Yves Thériault—who, like Roy, died in 1983—is a writer whose work has been closely associated with the Far North and especially the Inuit. *Agaguk* (1958), *Tayaout, fils d'Agaguk* (1969), and

Agoak, l' héritage d' Agaguk (1975)/*Agoak: The Legacy of Agaguk* form a quasi-trilogy that spans the period 1958 to 1975. Treating the conflict between Inuit and white society, Thériault moves into the sub-genre of adventure novels with his stress on atavistic violence; the last two of the group obviously play, in their titles, on the commercial success of the first. Thériault, who once said that 'books are merchandise that one has to sell', clearly banked on the 'exoticism' of the milieus of these novels for his Quebec/Canadian, and especially international, readers. Nevertheless his natural talent as a storyteller are undeniable, and made him, according to André Carpentier, the most read, most translated, and most republished Québécois author.

Agaguk, his most popular novel, is the story of a young Inuit of the Labrador-Ungava peninsula who finds intolerable the corruption and skulduggery of his father, the 'tribal chief' Ramook. He thus decides to take the orphan, Iriook, as his wife and move from the village to the tundra, where the two start a new life away from their community. It is far from peaceful. Finding that the illicit trader, Brown, has stolen his fur pelts, Agaguk sets fire to his hut and the thief burns to death. Ramook—fearing interference with his immoral and illegal activities—kills the Mountie, Henderson, who comes to investigate Brown's death. During a violent encounter with a mythical white wolf that threatens the life of Agaguk's son, Tayaout, Agaguk is badly disfigured. When Ramook tries to pin the murder of Henderson on Agaguk, Iriook outwits the investigator, Scott, who eventually finds the real culprits, Ramook and his sidekick, the shaman Ghorok, who hang for their crime. Agaguk refuses offers to become 'chief', and continues to live apart with his wife and child. Soon Iriook is pregnant again. She gives birth, first to a girl whom Agaguk wants to kill 'instinctively'. Iriook threatens to shoot him unless he spares their daughter as atonement for killing Brown, and Agaguk gives in. Iriook immediately bears a twin son, thus 'compensating' her husband. The equality that had developed in their general existence—especially in their sexual life, in which pleasure was shared 'exceptionally' and was no longer the exclusive prerogative of the man—gives way at the end to a return to the more 'traditional' male hegemony.

Thériault skilfully develops the tension between the village and the tundra (shifting the action from one to the other), sustains suspense during the dramatic moments of the story, and arouses interest with the erotic content: *Agaguk* was one of the first Quebec novels after World War II to treat sex so explicitly. And there is an epic quality in the heroes' desperate struggle to survive the harsh Arctic elements, particularly the blizzards and the bitter cold. But unfortunately the author claims in a preliminary note that his novel is a 'documentary', set in a particular time (the 1940s) and place, though he distorts to the extreme Inuit mores and freely synthesizes behaviour patterns drawn from several centuries and widely separated areas. This distortion is notably evident in the treatment of anti-social acts ('The Inuk kills the way he loves . . .'), with theft, plundering, rape, and murder being attributed to 'atavistic forces' and interpreted as being part of the Inuit way of life. The 'automatic' killing of an infant female at birth is a constant refrain. Finally the social organization of Thériault's Inuit (grouped, like Amerindians, in tribes with chiefs), and their material culture, bear little if any resemblance to reality. Leaving this aside, the book has often been given an allegorical reading by critics, who see Thériault exploring the reality of Duplessis's Quebec through the Inuit and particularly the isolated micro-society formed by Agaguk, Iriook, and Tayaout (a reborn Quebec), and through the emphasis on sex (the liberation of a repressed society).

Tayaout is set mainly in Povungnituk, on the northeastern coast of Hudson Bay, and deals extensively with the Inuit soapstone-carving trade that developed there from the mid-nineteen fifties onwards. Iriook, who had forced her husband to honour a biblical conception of justice ('Thou shalt not kill'), here reverses herself, ordering her son to shoot Agaguk because he had violated a fundamental Inuit belief by selling his carvings to a white man. Thériault's Inuit, who are portrayed without sensitivity, are saddled with other asocial and violent behaviour and again automatically kill all female children at birth beyond the number required for the reproduction of the species.

Agoak (named for Agaguk's grandson) also begins in Povungnituk and follows the principal character to Frobisher Bay and later to the Far North, treating as well the computer revolution. Agoak works as an accountant in a bank at Frobisher Bay, having studied computer science in the South, following in his grandfather's footsteps by adopting the white man's commercial activities. But his wife Judith is raped by two American businessmen. Agoak goes into a frenzy, not only killing the two men, but amputating their sex organs. Formerly a model Inuit, Agoak now flees with Judith towards Ellesmere Island, where he performs more violence, killing in a most gruesome way a friendly family of four traditional Eskimos, two police officers, and his own newly born daughter. By entitling Agoak's two parts '*Les Esquimaux*' and '*Les Inuit*', Thériault is telling us that in the first the couple function according to white expectations, while in the second, after the initial crime, they revert to their original 'essence', again becoming 'the people'. While the author makes a pretence at 'balancing' the violence of Agoak by Judith's rape and by her husband's unmotivated references to 'the massacres in Viet Nam . . . by the Americans, those perfect white people', the outrages of Agoak weigh much more heavily on the reader, and the final result is a neo-colonialist discourse exceeded in its repugnance and ignorance only by Thériault's own comments on this third work: '. . . one might say that *Agoak* tends to prove that, under the civilized exterior, there is always a beast, a man in his brutish state . . . Agoak is an Eskimo . . . and he acts like an Eskimo . . . .'

Recent books on Thériault by Hélène Lafrance and André Carpentier have revealed hitherto unknown facts about his career that substantiate the critical view of his writing on the Inuit that I have been developing. He told Carpentier that he wrote *Agaguk* for the Paris publisher Grasset because the French 'seemed to know nothing about our indigenous peoples.' Yet he also admitted that the first version of that novel was set in the American South: 'The joke is that the original story took place in the bayous of Florida . . . But it's basically the same tale . . . Transpose it, take off for the Arctic, and you've got *Agaguk*.' Perhaps an explanation for the anthropological distortions of Thériault's Inuit cycle can be found in the unconscious tensions within him between the historical position of the Québécois as a dominated people, and their own responsibility, together with that of other whites, for the domination and oppression of aboriginal peoples.

In 1961 Thériault won the Governor General's Award for *Ashini (1960). Although the books centred on Agaguk and his descendants suggest that a sober reevaluation of the Inuit cycle is required, not all of Thériault's production, fortunately, is in that category. Ashini—one of his best and most popular works and the first to deal with Indians—is a short novel that has been described as an 'epic poem' and a 'lyrical meditation'. It is the supposed testament, written on birchbark, of an old Montagnais chief before his suicide. His daughter had abandoned the traditional life and two of his sons and his wife were dead. His plan to liberate his people had met with little interest, and as for his plea to the Great White Father to meet him for a palaver, it had simply been ignored. He thus succumbed, officially, to 'mental derangement' and took his life. Ashini recounts the sacred origins of his people and the totemic struggle of the wolves in language steeped in natural images. Clearly Thériault, who claimed a Montagnais great-grandfather (another 'fact' questioned by his admirer, André Carpentier), wrote more positively and sympathetically about the Montagnais in Ashini— and in its female counterpart *N'tsuk (1968)—than about the Inuit.

Also outside the nationalist mainstream is **Jean Basile** (Bezroudnoff, b. 1932), who wrote a trilogy steeped in bohemian characters on their way to becoming part of the drug culture: La Jument des Mongols (The Mongols' Mare, 1964), Le Grand Khan (1967), and Les Voyages d'Irkoutsk (1970), all of which are untranslated. There is a certain cynical nihilistic register in Basile's writing—his main characters mock all forms of political commitment, especially that of the independence movement—and his long, meandering sentences without paragraphs, plus his use of collage and cinematic techniques, give it a certain modernist quality.

The love theme, treated in a blasé way by Basile, is approached quite differently by Claire Martin and Louise Maheux-Forcier, who created women characters with particular sensitivity some time before feminism developed into a movement. The bourgeois milieus of their novels are a far cry from Thériault's or Roy's northern frontiers, and from the collectivist preoccupations of the '*texte national*' that were contemporaneous with their works. Yet their opening up of taboo subjects, like extra-marital sexual relations and lesbianism, is not unconnected to the questioning of established norms and values that came with the Quiet Revolution.

Called by one critic 'our theoretician of the human heart', **Claire Martin** (the pseudonym of Claire Faucher, b. 1914) has excelled in treating psychological aspects of love relationships, and in diagnosing the Quebec bourgeois family and its institutional props, with courage and exactitude. She was also one of the pioneers, at the very beginning of the sixties, in the use of first-person narrative and shifting point of view, although her internal monologues are more 'descriptions of consciousness' (Robert Humphrey) than disjointed stream-of-consciousness structures. Her writings have generally been more concerned with the individual subject than with the contextual macro-society, but her outstanding autobiography implicitly yet powerfully links the particular with the general.

Martin's first novel, *Doux-amer* (1960)/*Best Man*, is narrated by the publisher/editor and sometime lover of Gabrielle Lubin, a novelist and dramatist with whom he has had a long liaison. Gabrielle 'lays claim to her rights to freedom by putting her career before love, by allowing herself to be unfaithful, and by marrying a man younger than herself—all time-honoured actions and privileges reserved for men' (Nicole Bourbonnais). Thus traditional roles are reversed and the narrator becomes 'the Other—submissive, faithful, devoted'. The break between the narrator and the writer occurs after the success of Gabrielle's first play, when she meets the attractive (but mediocre) journalist and actor Michel Bullard, with whom she falls passionately in love. His manipulativeness and unfaithfulness, however, lead to a marital crisis that is 'resolved' by Michel's death in a car accident, giving the former lover hope that a reconciliation is possible. A second perspective arises from the manuscript that Gabrielle offers the publisher in which he reads her lucid analysis of the same events. Self-reflexive observations on the art of writing are also innovative for the time.

The twenty-six sequences of *Quand j'aurai payé ton visage* (1962) / *The Legacy* are composed for the most part of the monologues of Catherine, and her brother-in-law and future lover Robert, with a few belonging to Mme Ferny, mother of the latter and of Bruno. There is thus a variable internal focus on the three. Catherine and Robert, a performer and song-writer (the French title is that of the emblematic song he writes for his beloved), meet at the engagement party of Catherine and Bruno, and are irresistibly drawn to one another. Each of the recurring monologues is introduced by the capitalized name of the 'speaker', and encapsulates varying perspectives on the central adulterous event. The whole gives a critical portrait of an upper-class Quebec family for whom wealth alone counts, a milieu dominated by shabby class and ethnic prejudices.

Martin's most important literary achievement was undoubtedly her brilliant and moving two-volume autobiography, *Dans un gant de fer: I. La Joue gauche* (1965) and *II. La Joue droite* (1966), translated as *In an Iron Glove* (1973) and *The Right Cheek* (1975). Although evidently non-fiction memoirs (the original publications carried no generic designation), they read like novels and in fact *La Joue droite* won the Governor General's Award for fiction! The books cover the first twenty-six years in Claire Faucher's life, from her birth in 1914 until 1940. The first was an immediate success, but also caused controversy for its frank and impassioned stripping bare of the familial, educational, and social underside of the author's well-to-do Quebec City family. The style combines harmoniously a piquant yet sombre humour, social satire, and tragic exposé, and the reader is delighted by the lively repartee and crystallized wisdom gleaned from often humiliating and painful experiences, in the manner of the classical moralists. The first volume follows Claire from birth to age thirteen, when her long-suffering mother died, leaving the child frightened before the monstrous figure of her father, mysogynistic in the extreme with regard to his spouse and five daughters and for whom the 'love' of a woman for her husband meant 'submission, subjection and servility'. The second volume traces Claire's long and difficult road towards autonomy as her doddering father becomes more and more ridiculous. In the midst of this jungle of human sentiments stands the cheerful strength and independence of the narrator's maternal grandmother. (Her solidity, like that of her unlikely contemporary, Grand-Mère Antoinette of Blais's *Une Saison*, makes one speculate about the reasons for the weakness of the female offspring of the next generation. Might one suggest that this is related to the defeat of the liberal-democratic movement around the time of Confederation?) Claire Martin is particularly admired for her forthright condemnation of the ambient xenophobia of her own milieu—which included anti-Semitism that also afflicted other sections of Canadian society during the Depression years.

Louise Maheux-Forcier (b. 1929), also a product of an upper-class family with socio-cultural taboos similar to those that plagued Claire Martin, produced a trilogy based on the socially proscribed urge of her characters to create unisexual feminine unions, usually closely linked to epiphanous childhood memories and in reaction to vulgar and insensitive men. *Amadou* (1963), *L'Ile joyeuse* (1965)/*Isle Of Joy* (1987), and the prize-winning *Une forêt pour Zoé* (1969) / *A Forest for Zoë*—all marked by the author's musical and artistic background—are in fact three variations on a theme.

Amadou begins with the dramatic announcement that the narrator, Nathalie, has killed her husband Julien, an alcoholic painter and art teacher. Through memory she reconstitutes an exchange of heterosexual partners in the abandoned Romanesque chapel in Normandy when she became magnetically drawn to Sylvia. Her secret correspondence with the latter, discovered by Julien, led to his violent destruction of her letters and the subsequent tragedy. But further back in Nathalie's memory is the radiant lyrical adolescent figure of Anne, a waif her mother once brought to the family's home who died by drowning, perhaps suicidally. *L'Ile joyeuse* centres on another triangle made up of Isabelle, her musical colleague Stéphane, who hides his marriage from her, and his mistress Julie. Again the male drinks excessively and lacks tenderness, but Julie offers an image of independence and freedom that Isabelle associates with dream-like visions of music and birds, and with an enchanted isle of sand. The most accomplished of the three works is *Une forêt pour Zoé*. Thérèse is trying to write a novel based on her first amorous experience as an adolescent, twenty years earlier, with her red-headed, green-eyed friend Zoé. Her obsession with the girl prevents her from advancing with her book and from carrying on the routine of daily life. Caught between reality and dream, between the adult present of the narration and the childhood of her memories, repelled by the brutal or indifferent men she has known, she is haunted by visions of the girls and women—all with physical features like Zoé's and substitutes for her—to whom she has been sexually attracted. Maheux-Forcier here composes a complex and poetic plot in which erotic memories are painted in the delicate semitones of impressionism, and an inherent musicality lends grace and shading not only to the content but also to the phrasing, pitch, and tonality of the writing.

Martin and Maheux-Forcier might be considered proto-feminists. The charges they level against men are not systematized. They do not occupy the entire fictional space, nor are they extended to the entire male sex, as will often be the case in many of the works to be considered in the next chapter.

4

THE EMERGENCE OF THE FEMINIST 'I'

It is generally agreed that the most notable development in Québécois literature in the 1970s was the emergence of feminist writing. The introduction to Volume V (1970-1975) of the *Diction-naire des oeuvres littéraires du Québec* states that 'audacious and inventive women who were in love with words and were assiduous readers of texts of other women from here or elsewhere whose destiny resembled theirs, realized that it was henceforth possible for them to break the silence and proclaim their "femininity" and desire for freedom.' I shall examine here a representative selection of feminist novels before covering other novels of the seventies in the next chapter.

Influenced by women essayists and creative writers in France and the United States, but at the same time reflecting critically on their own specific history and socio-cultural evolution, Nicole Brossard, Louky Bersianik, Madeleine Gagnon, Jovette Marchessault, France Théoret, Yolande Villemaire and others have made original contributions over the last fifteen years to both the form and content of the novel. Their appearance on the literary horizon was closely linked to parallel developments that included the or-ganization of militant women's groups demanding to be heard on questions affecting their lives; the launching of new feminist journals (*Québécoises deboutte!*, *Les Têtes de pioches*, *Des luttes et des rires*, *La Vie en rose*); the creation of drama companies (Le Théâtre des cuisines and Le Théâtre expérimental des femmes); the Théâtre du Nouveau-Monde's strongly feminist collective productions of *La Nef des sorcières/A Clash of Symbols*, Denise Boucher's *Les Fées ont soif/The Fairies Are Thirsty*, and Jovette Marchessault's *La Saga des poules mouillées/The Saga of the Wet*

Hens; and the founding of two publishing houses dedicated to women's writing, Les Editions de la Pleine Lune and Les Editions du Remue-ménage. In 1975 the modernist literary journal *La Nouvelle Barre du jour* launched the first of its annual issues devoted to women's writing, and the more traditional review, *Liberté*, sponsored an international conference on the theme 'Women and Writing'. That same year almost half the novels published in Quebec were written by women. Of these, critics considered three-quarters to be among the most important in that genre.

In a 1986 essay, France Théoret—who, like most of the writers mentioned above, has combined creative writing with theoretical considerations, often combining the two—distinguished between 'feminist writing', 'feminine literature', and 'writing in the feminist mode'. The first, according to her classification, concerns essays, manifesto-like texts, and personal testimonies; the second, simply 'women's writing', but writing that doesn't challenge feminine stereotypes; the third, sometimes designated as 'fiction', is consciously feminist, proposes the emergence of a feminine 'subject', and challenges patriarchal language structures and traditional genres. Patricia Smart, less rigid in her divisions, treats positively other writers like Germaine Guèvremont, Gabrielle Roy, and Anne Hébert, all of whom rejected the consecrated image of woman as *mater dolorosa*, as sex-object, or solely as the reproducer of the species.

Feminist writers, who began to create their own institutional infrastructures, treated the feminine condition openly; they wrote of the body, lesbianism, heterosexual relations, and language, and developed a feminist literary theory. As **Nicole Brossard** (b. 1943) said in *L'Amèr; ou le chapitre effrité* (1977) / *These Our Own Mothers; or The Disintegrating Chapter*: 'To write *I am a woman* has serious consequences.' In another text she said that for a woman, writing is even more important than speaking because by writing 'woman' she leaves a concrete mark in the form of a book, 'enters public and private space . . . and becomes a part of History.'

After her first foray into the novel form with *Un Livre* (1970)/*A Book*, Brossard continued with *Sold out: Étreinte/illustration*

(1973) / *Turn of a Pang*, and *French kiss*: *Étreinte/exploration*
(1974) / *French Kiss; or A Pang's Progress*. In each of these books
the stress was on a novel-in-the-making, on process rather than
product. The twenty-one divisions of *French kiss*—each designated by the noun '*fois*' (times), preceded by a number—plus the
several addenda, suggest many attempts at creating a more or less
coherent text, and are set off against three boxed chapters in larger
bold-face type, with the last sentences often written in by hand.
These boxed chapters, interspersed with reflections on the process
of writing, are more traditional in style and, as Pierre Nepveu has
suggested, seem to signify that the novel in its consecrated form
is perceived by Brossard as being 'other', alien to her purpose. In
French kiss and her other texts there is a clear distancing of the
confused narrative voice from history, society, the outer world,
representation.

Although the 'action' of *French kiss* is clearly set in Montreal,
and there is an abundance of *joual* expressions and distinct references to the linguistic tensions in that city, there is also a nearly
complete break with psychology and character. There are five
designated persons—Camomille Delphie, Lucy Savage, Marielle
Desaulniers, called Elle by her brother Alexandre (Lexa), and his
friend Georges. Nepveu refers to Marielle as the narrator, another
critic gives this role to Lucy, but the author throws the reader off
by referring to a masculine '*narrateur*'. In any case Marielle, her
hair dyed blue, driving her mauve 1965 Plymouth convertible from
the east end of Sherbrooke St to the west and back, is certainly at
the centre of the 'story', which develops from, and interweaves
with, the '*étreinte*' (embrace)/exploration of the book's subtitle,
the first part of which generates the erotic lesbian relationship
between Camomille and Lucy and incestuous pulls between Elle and
Lexa. 'Exploration' is clearly a clue to the book's probing of the
creative process through a form of automatic writing. The terms
'embrace' and 'exploration' recur throughout *French kiss*; there
are ample self-reflexive references to text, fiction, page, paper,
narration, grammar, syntax; and the ambivalent word '*langue*'
(tongue, language) bridges the two components of the subtitle.
History appears in fleeting references to Marie de l'Incarnation,

Jeanne Mance, a rape that occurred in 1689, the crushing of French forces during the Battle of the Plains of Abraham, the fur trade, and 'La Corriveau'— Marie-Josephte Corriveau, who lived near Quebec City and was executed in 1763 for murdering her second husband. Her skeleton was displayed publicly in a cage to deter others from doing the same, and she has become a symbolic figure of female resistance to male hegemony in the writings of a number of leading feminists.

In *L'Amèr; ou le chapitre effrité* Brossard, like other feminist writers, attacks frontally the delimiting reproductive role attributed to women in a traditional male-dominated society, weaving variations on the title, which combines the senses of *la mère* (mother) and *l'amer/l'amère* (bitter), through additional references such as *la mer* (sea), *l'amer* (seamark), the enigmatic *l'amer-mort* (which may be a play on *la Mer morte* (the Dead Sea), and the Scottish *Lammermoor*). The author proclaims: *J'ai tué le ventre et fait éclater la mer* (I have killed the belly and made the sea/mother explode). The narrator's father and mother are designated anonymously as '*lui*' and '*elle*'. Brossard—again resorting to a form of automatic writing, but one that has a distinct feminist and lesbian orientation—flays, in manifesto-like fashion, the 'patriarchal' mothers and daughters, those '*clownes maternelles*' who live only for men and have nothing to offer each other but their '*silence domestique*'. She also displays her lesbianism and dreams of women procreating women alone.

A year before the publication of *L'Amèr*, **Louky Bersianik** (Lucille Durand, b. 1930) stunned the reading public and the literary community of Quebec with her *L'Euguélionne* (1976)/*The Euguelionne: a Triptych Novel*. The title, of Greek origin, means 'the woman who brings the news'—a sort of extra-terrestrial female Christ-figure who ostensibly visits Earth in search of a man of her 'species', and ends up rallying women to fight against their imposed inferiority. This solid book explodes the concept of genre by combining novel, essay, anthology of prose poems, satire, parody, science-fiction, manifesto, academic thesis replete with learned notes, dictionary of feminized neologisms, code of ethics, collection of maxims, and manual of (especially) female sexuality.

It brilliantly mixes humour (mainly puns and the transformation of consecrated sayings, slogans, and clichés) with serious reflections on war, colonialism, and exploitation. Bersianik's opus, while uncompromisingly feminist, is not marked by the bare rage of other writings in the same vein. Its approach to sexual relations, though highly critical of historical and contemporary practice, is essentially a reposed and heterosexual one that ends with an appeal for an alliance between women and men to redeem the humanity of both. It does, however, excoriate the practices of clitoridectomy and infibulation.

As in many other contemporary novels, especially feminist ones, *L'Euguélionne* contains a plethora of literary, artistic, and musical references that traverse the entire text. The 'extra-terrestrial' heroine certainly is well versed in earthly cultural signposts. Her wide-ranging allusions include important Quebec names like the ubiquitous La Corriveau, Rodolphe Girard's Marie Calumet, Anne Hébert's 'La Fille maigre' (Skinny Girl), Antonine Maillet's 'La Sagouine', Marie-Claire Blais's Pauline Archange, Réjean Ducharme's Bérénice and Chateaugué, Émile Nelligan (a favourite reference of Quebec feminists), André Langevin, Gilles Vigneault, Raoul Duguay, Raymond Lévesque, legendary trade-unionist Madeleine Parent, and Henri Bourassa. Another implied source seems to be the Quebec *automatiste* poet and playwright Claude Gauvreau, whose '*exploréen*' language has perhaps influenced the elaborate use of proper names in Bersianik's work. A host of French writers are evoked, from Rabelais to Sartre and Simone de Beauvoir. The eighteenth-century feminist revolutionary Olympe de Gouges also appears. Cervantes, Nietzsche, Jiri Hajek (*The Good Soldier Schweik*), Lewis Carroll, Joyce, Shakespeare, the Brontë sisters, and Virginia Woolf (another oft-cited figure in feminist works) also crop up. Classical female figures like Antigone, Electra, and Lysistrata surface too. (Bersianik's subsequent novel, *Le Pique-nique sur l'Acropole* (1979), is in fact set in antiquity and is a feminist pastiche of Plato's *The Banquet*.)

L'Euguélionne seems to have anticipated (or influenced) key aspects of Denys Arcand's films *Le Déclin de l'empire américain* and *Jésus de Montréal*: in the first, the sexual conquests of the history professor, Rémi, and his chronic infidelity; in the second, the scene in which a future woman 'disciple' of Christ is asked to bare her chest for a TV beer commercial. In Bersianik's book there is also an audition for a beer commercial for a product called 'Taball Zingande-et-une' (read Labatt Fifty-one!), with similarly humiliating 'artistic' directions to the actress. There are also pastiches of Genesis (the narrator searches in vain for Adam's uterus) and the Sermon on the Mount; prime targets are Sigmund Freud and French psychoanalyst Jacques Lacan, who appear as 'Saint Sigmund' and 'Saint Jacques Linquant', the latter name evoking '*délinquant*' and '*clinquant*'—flashy (Maroussia Ahmed). Freud's theory of 'penis envy' is uproariously torn to shreds, and Descartes's 'Cogito, ergo sum' becomes: '*Je bande, donc je suis*'! (I get an erection, therefore I exist), in a general demythologization of male sexual/political hegemony. And the Catholic Church is not spared. Anti-abortionists are satirized ('The foetus is a citizen like any other'), clerics are given names like 'Saint Francis Capricioso', and the Immaculate Conception becomes, in turn, '*l'émasculée conception*' (emasculated conception) and '*la maculée conception*' (stained conception). The play with language and spelling is often brilliant, as in the beautiful term '*enfaon*' (a combination of child and fawn), and in phrases like '*Nous fûmes alors prises d'une* envie *phormidable non de phallus mais de phourire*' (We were overtaken then by a great *desire* not for a phallus but for mad laughter) the author plays humorously on the presence in French of words of Latin and Greek origin, sometimes rendering the /f/ sound by 'ph'. Like other feminist writers, Bersianik attacks sexually 'liberated' males and rebellious hippies who exploit women nearly as much as their 'repressed' and 'straight' fellows. All in all, *L'Euguélionne* is a veritable *tour de force*.

Lueur. Roman archéologique (1979) by **Madeleine Gagnon** (b. 1938) has a more serious tonality and is more poetic in its language. As with Bersianik, the merging of genres is a conscious aim of Gagnon, who sees her text as embracing poetry, the essay, and the novel. In fact aesthetic self-reflexivity is a constant preoccupation and links up with Nicole Brossard's central concerns. This self-conscious aspect includes the evocation of other writers and an 'archeological' element, emblazoned in the subtitle. It is concerned with memory, psychological drives, and the unconscious. At the heart of *Lueur* is a rehabilitation of the female lineage of the narrator-author, recalling the feminist slogan 'Our mothers are our sisters'. The narrator fantasizes her mother's congress with her father ('sweet night of my mother's loving perspiration') and her own birth ('isle of dreams, was it then my mother's belly?'), with its attendant coma and sedative and the hope that perhaps 'this cold burning will carry her off outside these walls of daily drudgery, far from the dull repetition of household chores, of nourishing . . .' The grandmother, of Gaspé fisherfolk stock, emerges as a towering figure who inspires the narrator-author, leaving her a heritage to cherish, but also traps to avoid. Weaving back and forth between first- and third-person, the narrative voice heeds the old lady's command: 'You must write, write me, take me into your words.' She, like the narrator's mother, had her crosses to bear, and the narrative voice generalizes: 'Each woman hushed her misery, alibi children, prison homes, muted rapes, absolved murders wedded to your tenacious grief, strange wishes, wishes of slaves with invisible chains.' The title *Lueur* (glimmer) suggests a ray of hope, in contrast with the implication of the epigraph that the archaeologist appears only when a culture can no longer defend itself. It is as if, in Patricia Smart's words, writing '*son histoire à elle*' (herstory)—as opposed to '*son histoire à lui*' (his(s)tory)—will offset the pessimism encoded there.

Almost in answer to Brossard's interrogation of the relationship between the real and the fictional, *Lueur* contains aggressive statements against the realistic aesthetic. Gagnon writes: 'I invent nothing . . . I write.' She adamantly refuses to reproduce 'the fraudulent writing of make-believe', opting rather for 'the time and space between emptiness, the places between the holes . . . oasis-words'. The truth, she says, leads directly to its own story-form; the story to its truth.

Like other feminist and generally experimental writers, Gagnon creates neologisms—as in her expression '*paroles désiliriantes*', the adjective combining '*désir*', '*délire*' (delirium), and '*riantes*' (laughing)—and feminizes genders of certain nouns that are masculine in French ('*espace*', '*exile*', '*insterstice*', '*antre*' (lair), and '*dynosaure*'), suggesting the feminine specificity of certain kinds of physical and psychological space, as well as rebelling against the monopolization of species by the male designation—just as the Euguélionne rejected the veiling of women's identity by the lack of distinction between man (gender) and man (species) in conventional discourse.

Nous parlerons comme on écrit (1982) / (We Shall Speak as One Writes) by **France Théoret** (b. 1942) is a largely autobiographical narrative that also has many poetic elements. The title evidently originated in a pronouncement the author heard as a little girl in the schoolyard from a companion who shared with her a love of language, coupled with a consciousness of speaking badly—part of Théoret's heritage of her rural petty-bourgeois milieu. The two children aimed at speaking in the lofty tones of the class dictations recited by their teacher-nun. The narrator's schoolfriend says: '. . . we shall keep an eye on words, we shall be their watchguards.' The narrator's identification with the doll of her first storybook, Ninon, is full of sensitivity, word-play, and muted revolt: 'I am a dispossessed plaything . . . the envelope of a tragi-comedy . . . If I say neither, not ['*ni non*'], I make clear that I do not say no and do not say yes.' Later the narrator, now a schoolteacher herself in the working-class area of Pointe Saint-Charles in Montreal, gives in to routine and a mechanical commitment to her job, and her reading and speech are characteristically affected: 'I no longer read nor write letters . . . I speak less and less.' Elsewhere she refers to herself as 'a woman born without a tongue, destined for silence and obedience', and the reference to obedience is a leitmotiv of the entire book.

The central theme of feminist revolt is expressed in the narrator's reflections on her upbringing—her relegation to serving rude and unkempt men in the family's grocery-store/tavern, her father's scorn for her interest in studying classical languages and mathematics, her mother's confusing and primitive advice about sexuality, the nuns' lurid warnings about 'sin', her abysmal first sexual experience at the hands of a persistent, boorish mate, and her legal exclusion from her father's will because of her sex. But even more, this revolt is expressed through the complementary narrative of an anonymous nurse, who recounts her experiences of more than thirty years in an obstetrics ward.

The unnamed 74-year-old nurse recounts to the main persona crucial and extraordinary, yet believable, incidents of tragic womanhood that she has observed throughout her life and career and reappears on eight occasions as an auxiliary narrator. (Théoret also evokes at least three times the narrator's traumatic childhood fall on a major Montreal street. She treats the incident both literally and symbolically, as in this sentence in which she recalls her interest in certain school subjects, ridiculed by her father: 'What is left of Latin and Mathematics since my head crashed down on the pavement that May morning?') Especially striking are the nurse's stories about women transformed into tortured, strange beings because of their harrowing marital experiences. One turned mute because her husband threw her out of the house while pursuing their eighteen-year-old daughter; she grew progressively fatter until she 'burst' and died at forty-eight. Another's resistance took the form of sleeping twenty hours a day before succumbing to mental illness. Marriage is consequently seen by the narrator as 'fatigue duty by day and especially by night'. The nurse strongly inspires in her a desire to fight against established codes and practices and assert her autonomy: 'I must take apart, stone by stone, the edifice that gives . . . power to some while letting others dance around its walls.' She draws sustenance from other women, especially the auxiliary narrator, and says: 'Women can breathe, thanks to other women.'

Another subject of attack is what the narrator perceives as the leftist dogmatism of fellow-teachers. Some teachers'-union debates are described as 'projected goulags', for there is talk of purges, and the label '*bourgeois*' is stuck on recalcitrant members. Thus, although ideological evolution in Quebec is generally seen as positive—the end of clerical domination, the rise of new communities and new autonomous forces, including the women's movement—there is also the emergence of a Left, which, in the narrator's view, began by being libertarian then became authoritarian.

Théoret's social observations extend beyond the narrator's tense home surroundings to those of her teaching job in Pointe Saint-Charles—most of the forty little girls in her class come to school hungry and the schoolboys often suffer beatings at home—and to Mexico, where she travels from the capital to Vera Cruz. Noting the tin coca-cola signs on the rooftops of homes with their ragamuffin urchins, Théoret makes the ironic comment that more children work today for want of food than during the Industrial Revolution of the nineteenth century. In poetic prose she identifies with the Mexican people and their history: 'I am an Aztec dressed in a tortured skin . . . I speak Nahualt and survive reddened and ribbed at the foot of the phallic rocks of Tepoztlan.' Familiarizing herself with the paintings of Orozco, Rivera, Guerrero, Siqueiros, Maria Izquierdo, and Marta Palau, she sees their work as 'the hidden face of the other America, the one that is silent, the one I have not learned . . .' and adds this reflection: 'Self-centred North America, with its gaze turned towards Europe, has been built on the negation of the other Americas.'

There is in the text an alternation between more traditional narrative and the use of fragmented and syncopated techniques, and an unusual variation in the narrative voice (*je, on, elle(s), nous*). The poet and playwright Claude Gauvreau (1925-71) is a reference point (as in *Lueur*) because of his automatic writing (*l' exploréen*) and especially his suicide, which is linked to that of Hubert Aquin and tied closely to the tragic tonality of Théoret's text: 'My memory is on fire. The suicide of Gauvreau. The suicide of Aquin. Society's suicides.' (Gauvreau was a signator of the landmark avant-garde, anti-authoritarian manifesto, *Refus global* (Total Rejection), 1948.) That other recurring figure among feminist writers, La Corriveau, appears in striking images: 'I am suspended, alive, above the cemetery. I am La Corriveau still when night descends.' Liszt, Schönberg, Varese, and Mahler appear, the latter's *Kindertotenlieder* being an appropriate metaphor for Théoret's childhood and youthful angst.

In her 1986 essay already referred to, France Théoret criticizes certain formalist tendencies of modernist writing in Quebec for having reduced the narrative subject to 'a body, a textual presence abstracted from history.' She then projects the emergence of 'writing in the feminine that seeks to integrate the weight of reality into the reality of the text', and in which the 'family novel' and the 'social novel' confront one another, giving rise at their juncture to 'the feminine subject'. *Nous parlerons comme on écrit* is a fine attempt to effect such a fusion.

Jovette Marchessault was born in 1938 in the greater Montreal area, into a working-class family with Amerindian antecedents. At thirteen she was obliged to work in a textile factory, and then held a number of clerical jobs. She drew on these roots for her novel *La Mère des herbes* (1980)/*Mother of the Grass*—the second part of a proposed trilogy. (It began with *Comme une enfant de la terre* (1975) / *Like a Child of the Earth*, which won the Prix France-Québec.) *La Mère des herbes* has been called 'a harsh and beautiful book' because of its condemnation, on the one hand, of male dominance and especially of clerical control, and on the other its celebration of the matriarchal heritage. This lyrical hymn to life and creativity was dedicated by Marchessault to her mother, and celebrates the goddesses of Amerindian mythology. Like Brossard and Gagnon, Marchessault dreams of solely feminine reproduction of the species. The narrator's childhood on the St Lawrence is a paradise lost ('A million bees lap up the liqueur of clover'), which remains imbedded in her memory once she moves into the heart of the working-class city. She has memories of 'Belle-Béatrice', who sang in many tongues, and especially of her grandmother, who tells her: 'One day you'll see that there is more blood in a woman's body than water in a lake.' Although they live at the edge of Montreal island, the narrator's family is never far from the odours of the oil refineries. Grandma works in furs, and mother in chocolate and textiles in spring and summer, while the men are employed in a munitions plant. And Marchessault evokes with great force the wounded and mutilated of the war.

Various women from Quebec's history—Marie de l'Incarnation, Marguerite Bourgeoys, Madeleine de Verchères, Jeanne Mance, and Kateri Tekakwita—fill the imagination of the narrator. With the end of the war comes unemployment and misery for the family, who are obliged to move to the heart of the city and live in dingy quarters. The narrator, too, must now seek work in various sombre and unhealthy plants, and later as an encyclopedia saleswoman and eventually a bookstore clerk. She travels the continent on Greyhound buses, picking up odd jobs, reaching as far as Yucatan, while discovering her lesbian inclinations.

The text is divided into seven '*chants*' of unequal quality. In the fourth and last, among the most impressive, the description of the grandmother's departure from earth is very moving. Marchessault represents another variant of the feminist writer who not only weds autobiography, myth, and symbolism, but achieves a lyricism that flows out of her Amerindian heritage.

La Vie en prose (1980) by **Yolande Villemaire** (b. 1949) caused something of a sensation for its exuberance and formal experimentation. Its self-consciousness begins with the very title, variations of which traverse the novel's entirety in brilliant fashion, playing on the popular Edith Piaf song (*La vie en rose*) and a host of other connotations. It interweaves a novel-in-the-making; a journal; a collection of letters; fragments of conversation; reflections on writing, literature, and the counter-culture; and a heterogeneity of places and people.

The anecdotal aspect of the work is very tenuous—confused and confusing in its circularity. A certain Vava (Eva Vera Indian-napolis!) has the first and almost last (nearly identical, equally vague) word during a meeting of a women's editorial collective that is considering a manuscript for publication, submitted by a certain 'Noémie Artaud'. A report on this is being prepared by one of the central 'characters', Nane Yelle, whose 'real' name is Noé Vladimira Yelle, although she is also referred to as Danielle Yelle. It is never clear whether Nane is a character in a novel being written by Solange Tellier or Thériault, or one of the other 'characters' of *La Vie en prose*, or is a character of the aforementioned novel itself. Perhaps she is all three. At one point the narrator of *La Vie en prose* attributes to herself an unrequited passion that obsesses Nane. The profusion of characters in the women's collective, many of them bearing anagrammatic names (Nane-Anne, Alice-Celia, Laure-Aurel), evokes the following comment from Pierre Nepveu: '. . . the frenzy of proper nouns in

Villemaire becomes a veritable sign of an impossible appropria-
tion of reality . . . they indicate only an identity, but one that is
always provisional, ephemeral, substitutive.'

Nepveu sees Villemaire and other writers of the seventies and
eighties as products of an environment in which there is a loss of
the sense of history, where reality is elusive, the territory of culture
fragmented, and feelings of collective solidarity are breaking
down or being redefined. In *La Vie en prose* this is evident in the
higgledy-piggledy juxtaposition of events in California, New
York, Provence, Rome, Arizona, Britain, Mexico, Egypt, with
those closer to home: Montreal, the author's native Saint-Augus-
tin, Lévis, Gaspé, Berthier, Pont-Viau, La Malbaie, and the Ile
d'Orléans; and in the eccentric linking of such names as Rosa
Luxembourg and Marilyn Monroe. Real events—the Montreal
Olympics of 1976, the assassination of Italian premier Aldo Moro,
the death of John Diefenbaker—are inserted into the trials and
tribulations of the fictional women mentioned above.

Conversations are reported in direct and indirect style, and most
often in hyper-*joual*, with some humorous turns of phrase that play
on the ambiguity of unassimilated borrowings from English: '*Elle
a réussi à mettre la grippe sur sa vie*' (She succeeded in getting a
grip [*grippe* = a cold] on her life), '*Elle twinkelle des yeux*',
'*scotch-tapée sur le mur*', with many uses of 'switch', 'punch',
'trip', and 'anyway'. This self-deprecating look at popular
Québécois speech is coupled with grave quotations from Émile
Nelligan and, more often, parodic puns on lines from Réjean
Ducharme, Claude Gauvreau, Hubert Aquin, and others. References to literature are, in fact, nearly inexhaustible, ranging
through Quebec writing (from Laure Conan to Michel Tremblay)
to French and European authors (from Lamartine to Michel Tour-
nier, and Shakespeare to Brecht), to Americans (Burroughs,
Ginsburg, Poe, Timothy Leary), to Marquez and Castaneda, and
to feminists (Sylvia Plath, Virginia Woolf, Kate Millett, Gertrude
Stein, and Anaïs Nin). Feminism, however, is just one minor
component in a heterogeneous framework of cultural and socio-
political references of great variety (illustrating what Pierre Nepveu calls the '*fragmentation du territoire de la culture*'). This

distinguishes Villemaire from the other writers discussed above, with the possible exception of the early Nicole Brossard. Villemaire's concerns are more counter-cultural than feminist.

Nepveu views the discontinuity of Villemaire's text as being related to a situation 'in which meaning is everywhere and nowhere, and values and non-values tend to merge or eliminate one another.' He sees Villemaire's writing—like that of Hubert Aquin, Nicole Brossard, and Réjean Ducharme—as being marked by what he calls 'writing/culture of form/energy rather than form/meaning'.

The feminist writers discussed in this chapter have clearly shaken institutionalized patriarchy in Quebec and helped change the contours of its literary/cultural landscape. They have exceeded the bounds of literary conventions in new ways and have brought to the forefront of current Québécois literature new subject-matter and new ways of seeing and expressing the particular desires and sentiments of their sex. They have revitalized genres and forms, whether their tonality has been satirical or grave or counter-cultural. Their creativity has been affected by pervasive cultural trends emanating from beyond the borders of Quebec as well as by a certain depoliticization within it. As a result, their denunciation of women's oppression, of that of colonial peoples of the Americas, of wars and exploitation (especially in the writing of Bersianik, Gagnon, Théoret, and Marchessault), has usually occurred without questioning the foundations of the dominant socio-economic system—unlike Gabrielle Roy, for example, in her Montreal novels.

5

THE LAST TWENTY YEARS

THE SEVENTIES: A DIVERSITY OF VOICES

Obviously referring to the 1970 October Crisis and the 1980 referendum on sovereignty-association, Andrée Ferretti described the seventies in these dire words: 'Beginning with repression and ending in sadness, the decade could be summed up in one word: misfortune.' In the middle of these two momentous events there was the unexpected electoral victory of the Parti Québécois in November 1976, which was cheered by most creative writers and artists. The decade at first did not mark a sharp break with the preceding one, in which the politicization of the novel was an important trend. As it went on, however, there was a certain inward-turning by many writers, with more concern for the micro- rather than the macro-society. As Jean-François Chassay has put it, there began a substantial shift from *le pays* (the land) to *le paysage* (the landscape, or the immediate surroundings of everyday life), which has continued to the present.

In the midst of these developments, the language issue—as always—was central. In creative writing, political disquiet gave way to a preoccupation with the differentiation between, and respective status of, 'French French', Quebec popular speech, and *joual*.

Statistics show that from the mid-1960s on, the novel form replaced poetry as the dominant literary mode, judging by the number of titles published, the print-run of each title, and the reception of critics and public. During the past twenty years, for example, the number of novels published annually has quadrupled, and the thematic and formal gamut is very wide. It is therefore difficult to single out one or two, or even a handful of, currents and approaches.

The expansion of the novel, however, created a paradox when the growing literary 'institution'—publishers, marketing and promotion, criticism, teaching—indirectly exerted certain limitations, for commercial reasons, on its free expression. Jacques Godbout wittily saw the 'poet's' [read 'writer's'] evolution thus: 'The poet once held in his hands a lyre, then a rifle; today it's an attaché-case.' In the seventies a marked change also took place in university and college curricula, with the increasing inclusion of, and eventually entire programs on, home-grown literature. This created a substantial additional market.

In the light of the huge increase in the publication of novels in the seventies and eighties, this chapter must be very selective in its discussion of works and authors (some of whom achieved prominence earlier).

Anne Hébert (b. 1916) was for many years known mainly as one of Quebec's most distinguished poets. She began writing short prose fictions in the late 1930s and the 1940s that were collected in *Le Torrent* (1950). Her first novel, *Les Chambres de bois* (1958) / *The Silent Rooms* was followed over a decade later by the work that brought her to the fore of Quebec novelists, **Kamouraska* (1970). Between then and 1988 four more novels confirmed that in all her fiction Hébert employs a consummate literary skill to create a new and compelling reality of her own, using elements of folktale and Gothic romance and a unique ability to transform human frailties and passion, and the subservience of women, into fable or tragedy.

Les Chambres de bois is a poetic novel (*roman-poème*) set in France, where it was written after Hébert won a Royal Society fellowship. It begins like a fairy tale in the mining region of northern France, where Catherine, a working-class girl, meets the lord of the manor and his son, Michel, a pianist and seeming Prince Charming, who marries her and takes her to the oppressive two 'wooden rooms' of the title—his apartment in Paris. When Michel's sister Lia joins them, Catherine withers in the enclosed, shuttered, dark, demented atmosphere as her husband re-establishes his childhood pact with his sibling. For Michel, Catherine becomes the devil as woman. Fragile and ill, she escapes to the sunny south, where she begins life anew with the gentle potter Bruno, returning her wedding band to Michel. Although localized far from Quebec, this novel could be read not only as a fable of emancipation but, as Maurice Émond has suggested, as an allegory of the stifling socio-cultural values of the Duplessis period, which, like the aristocratic family of the novel, was moribund when the work appeared.

Kamouraska, Hébert's most celebrated work, is based on an actual murder. On January 31, 1839 the brutal and profligate Antoine Tassy, seigneur of Kamouraska in the Lower St Lawrence region, is murdered by Dr George Nelson, lover of Tassy's wife, who persuaded him to commit the crime. He then flees to Vermont, while she is tried for complicity and imprisoned for a few months. She has three identities: Élisabeth d'Aulnières, her maiden name; Élisabeth Tassy after she marries Antoine at age sixteen; and Élisabeth Rolland, the name she acquired in her marriage of convenience to a wealthy Quebec City notary two years after the crime. This latter name is the one she bears in the fictional present, set nearly eighteen years after Tassy's murder, and it is associated with her sumptuous home on the rue du Parloir in Upper Town.

The conceptual time of the novel is a single stifling summer night during which Élisabeth, under sedation, seeks sleep on doctor's orders in the room of one of her maids after spending hours at the bedside of the dying Rolland. During her fitful slumber, tormented by her guilt in the death of Tassy and fearful that her dying husband may openly accuse her of involvement in it, she recreates in her drowsy mind the terrible events of the past, constantly delaying the detailed remembrance of the bloody deed that is the centre of her existence, as is also her passion for Nelson. (Anagrammatically one could read the novel's entire narrative program—passionate love and violent murder—in 'Kamouraska', for *amour* is clearly enclosed within it, leaving *K . . . aska* (*Qu'est-ce que (l')amour*? What is love?). One could also extrapolate *mour(r)ras*, framed by *ka . . . ka*, suggesting 'You shall die . . . excrement'.) In a sort of internal monologue, Élisabeth moves from present-day events to memories, sometimes confusing the two and almost always using the present tense for both. The beginning and end of the novel, briefly narrated in the third person, are related to the fictional present in the rue du Parloir, and it concludes with the dramatic irony of the words of the servant in whose room Élisabeth was resting: 'Look at how much madame loves monsieur! Look how she's crying . . .' Between these two nodal points the narrative voice varies from first to second person (singular and plural in French, when Élisabeth addresses herself with intimacy or at a greater distance), to third person when she externalizes reactions of others to her.

Feminists have taught us that the 'private' in terms of sexual politics is, in fact, 'political', and Élisabeth, who gave birth eleven times, laments: 'All I have been is a faithful belly, a uterus for producing children.' In addition, there is in the novel a subtle linguistic-nationalist undercurrent. English sentences and references—and especially the charge read against Élisabeth by the anglophone judge during her trial for homicide—break into her monologue (rendered in italics), disturbing the linguistic and typographic rhythm of the French narrative, and provoke ironic outbursts: '*The Queen! Toujours the Queen! C'est à mourir de rire.*' (You can die laughing.) The seemingly politically indifferent Élisabeth registers the fact that 'they're accusing you in a foreign tongue . . . .' And while at first, lost in her amorous passion, she is oblivious to the hanging of the Patriote leaders, later she compares their revolt to hers: 'I live in the midst of fever and dementia, like my native land.' Élisabeth at one and the same time exhibits a high degree of aristocratic *anglomanie* (by furnishing her home *à l'anglaise*, sending her two eldest sons to Oxford, being proud of the governor's compliments for her English pronunciation, and by her parallel mockery of the speech of the '*Canayens*'), and yet constantly expresses revulsion at the language in which she is accused of being an accomplice to the crime. It is as if she were experiencing a struggle between the nationalist super-ego and her anglomanic id, or perhaps the reverse, both basically showing a linguistic and political conflict that (like the feminist one) is 'historical' in the broadest sense.

At the same time *Kamouraska* vividly captures the flavour of 150 years ago as the background for a breathless, onrushing, romantic portrait of a woman consumed by grief and passion. The late Claude Jutra made a beautiful film of it in 1973, skilfully using white, black, red, and green—colours that are evoked in the text.

Les Enfants du sabbat (1975) / *Children of the Black Sabbath* counterpoises two physical/moral spaces: the hermetic atmosphere of the convent of the Ladies of the Precious Blood in Quebec City, where Sister Julie of the Trinity, a sorceress, lives; and a shanty in an isolated rural region where she and her brother Joseph, the children of sorcerers, grew up in an atmosphere of rituals and untrammelled sensuality. The childhood scenes are in flashback because Sister Julie is able to transport herself mentally into the past. She scandalizes the other nuns in the strict convent with her strange behaviour, and an unsuccessful attempt at exorcism is made. When she mysteriously becomes pregnant and the baby is allowed to die, the rebellious Julie flees the convent—to join a black-garbed figure (the Devil?). Another closed community—this time a Calvinistic, English-speaking, incest-ridden one in the Gaspé that strongly resembles the francophone milieus of her other novels—is the setting for *Les Fous de Bassan* (1982) / *In the Shadow of the Wind*. The screeching gannets of the title, a howling, mysterious wind, and the sound of the sea are background for the reconstruction through six narratives of the rape and murder of two cousins, Nora and Olivia, by another cousin, Stevens, in August 1936—two of the narratives by the spirit of Olivia and by the criminal in letters to an army buddy. It was made into a film, shot on the Ile Bonaventure, in 1986.

Le Premier Jardin (1988) / *The First Garden*, the author's most recent work, refers to an ironic lost paradise of childhood in Quebec City of an actress, established in France, who came home to play Beckett's *O les beaux Jours* (*Happy Days*) and to visit her daughter. Quebec releases a flood of memories relating to her whole life. As in other Hébert works, the heroine has several names—her stage name Flora Fontanges, her birth name, and the name that had been given her by the disagreeable Upper Town family she was adopted by to erase her Lower Town origins. These labels merge with names of some of the *Filles du roy* (the king's girls), who were sent from France by Louis XIV to give themselves to colonial soldiers and are evoked by street names—and with whom Flora identifies. They are constant reminders of exploited women, of whom Flora had once been one.

The long, singly focalized internal monologue technique that **Gérard Bessette**, another established writer, developed in *L' Incubation* was extended in *Le Cycle* (1971) / *The Cycle* by the use of single and double parentheses and dashes to reveal subconscious and repressed thoughts, and the physiological reactions they aroused. In addition, *Le Cycle* presents seven internal monologues in which various members of the family of the deceased Norbert Barré, an east-end Montreal insurance agent, reflect on their relations with him, as well as on their own lives and on the cycle of obsessions that pass from one generation to the next. Sexual obsessions dominate, and there are also frequent reflections on religion and flashes of ethnic prejudice and political and economic concerns. A fascinating work, *Le Cycle* sometimes errs in introducing far-fetched imaginative content (usually of a Freudian variety) into the monologues of some of the characters. One could also question the one-sided totalitarian vision the author presents of the Quebec independence movement.

Bessette achieved a real *tour de force* with his prehistoric novel *Les Anthropoïdes* (1977), not yet translated, about the epic struggle for survival of the Kalahoumes, which the author estimates took place 500 millennia ago. Its subtitle is *roman d'aventure(s)*, suggesting two levels of reading. The first—the *aventures*—has to do with the fighting hordes. The second is self-reflexive and relates to the process and forms of telling the epic story, for the novel is narrated by the adolescent Guito, who is preparing for the harrowing supreme test of recounting the saga of his people's origins and undaunted survival before he can be officially named a '*paroleur*', the perpetuator of their history and collective consciousness. Bessette wrote this novel in poetic prose, rhythmic and flowing, that is full of internal rhyme. Some of the turns of phrase have a Québécois ring; one is struck, at the book's very end, by the name 'Kébékouâ' given to the river of ancestral beginnings of the Kalahoumes.

In 1975 Bessette published *La Commensale* (The Female Table Companion), which was actually written more than ten years earlier, before *L'Incubation*. The narrator, the arithmomanic accountant Jérôme Chayer—who spends time in jail after assaulting his boss, and then decides to write up the events he has been recounting to the reader—resembles Hervé Jodoin both physically and emotionally. Yet *La Commensale* lacks the economy of *Le Libraire*, and in fact suffers from the very logorrhoea for which Chayer reproaches some of his interlocutors. The humour, however—mostly verbal, but also situational—is witty and often hilarious.

Bessette's *Le Semestre* (1979) appears to be much more profoundly autobiographical than his *Mes romans et moi*, which appeared the same year. Through a third-person form of internal monologue, we learn that a nearly sixty-year-old professor, creative writer, and critic, Omer Marin—the titles of whose works closely resemble those of Bessette—teaches Quebec literature (from a psychocritical viewpoint) at Princess University in Narcotown/Kingston (locus of the action of *L'Incubation*). The divorced Marin is at a crisis in his life and has serious doubts about the quality of his creative and critical writing, as well as his teaching, which may soon end if he takes early retirement. He is making notes on his recent experiences (including a brief sexual encounter with one of his students) for a future novel. He has spent a good part of the term analysing the 'primal scene' and other psychosexual aspects of *Serge d'entre les morts* (1976), a novel by **Gilbert La Roque** (1941-84), which he sees as that author's vehicle for self-analysis, just as *Le Semestre* is for Marin/Bessette. (La Roque's as yet untranslated novel is an excellent monologue in long, undulating, often incomplete sentences centred, as the title indicates, on a series of deaths that obsess the narrator, Serge—that of his father, his authoritarian grandmother, an aunt, and the symbolic one represented by the marriage of his cousin Colette, to whom he was strongly attracted sexually—and on the narrator's attempt to express their impact on him in words.) *Le Semestre* is a sort of novel-confession (it has also been called a novel-essay), with echoes of *L'Incubation* in its repetition of the refrain 'How can one tell?', and of *Le Cycle* in its parenthetical physiological notations. Although there is a certain lack of unity in *Le Semestre*, and some padding and boring passages, these are compensated for by important affective elements in Marin's treatment of his parents and in his doubts about the quality and durability of his creative, critical, and academic activities. There is, too—as is usual with Bessette—a good dose of social and political satire. But in the political theme one senses his ambivalence with regard to his identity as a Québécois living for years in an anglophone milieu, and a certain enduring nationalism (he sees Canada as 'two countries within one') that had obviously evolved since *Le Cycle* and includes admiration for René Lévesque following the Parti Québécois electoral victory of 1976. This novel is more than ever self-reflexive, with metafictional references to characters in other Bessette novels and repeated recollections of the tragic *dernier épisode* of Hubert Aquin's suicide two years before *Le Semestre* appeared.

The nationalist perspective is more salient in **André Langevin**'s *L'Élan d'Amérique* (1972, not translated), which was a major literary event when it appeared sixteen years after his previous novel. It is focused on two indirect internal monologues—that of Claire Peabody (née Boisvert, changed to Greenwood in the New England melting-pot), wife (and daughter!) of a wealthy but impotent vice-president of a US pulp-and-paper company with holdings in northern Quebec, and that of Antoine, a Québécois woodsman and guide—and is a profoundly pessimistic look at the survival of the francophone entity in the face of the massive US technological assault on traditional ways of making a living. The title refers both to the mythological elk (the *élan d'Amérique* that Claire wounds and her husband finishes off with his advanced rifle from aboard his Cessna), and the ironic sense of the irrepressible energy emanating from the US. The title also conveys sardonically the fate of Franco-Americans like Claire's prostitute mother, and of herself, who commits suicide—an implied warning of the possible fate of the Québécois.

In 1974 Langevin published *Une chaîne dans le parc/Orphan Street*, in which the traumatic orphan theme that haunted his first novels (and his own early years) resurfaced. It is the story of eight-year-old Pierrot, who spends a week in June 1944 with an uncle, his legal guardian, and his aunts after four frightful years in a Church-run orphanage where he escaped the cruel treatment of the nuns through dreams of the wonderful '*Homme bleu*' and the magical cat Balibou. Hoping for a friendly family environment in his relatives' working-class home, he finds instead only self-centredness, hypocrisy, and cruelty. Happily he finds solace with his red-headed neighbour Jane, who is about the same age; in visiting the park and the Lafontaine family nearby, who treat him as one of their own; and in thinking about a long silver chain, which reminds him of the sun, even though it represents violence. Twirled threateningly by its owner, Gaston (the Rat), it becomes 'a huge circle of light' to the boy. (Gaston uses it to injure a military policeman who is his rival for Isabelle Lafontaine, and the policeman kills him.) After eight days Pierrot leaves for a trade school, thinking that life outside the walls of the orphanage was not all that different from life inside. But as he is about to enter the confines of another institution, he has a store of good memories to comfort him—including Jane (whom he poetically refers to as his 'memory'), Mme Lafontaine (Maman Pouff), and the brilliance of the chain. Only gradually do we learn the identity of the 'he' (Pierrot) at the centre of the story, that Pierrot's father confined him to the orphanage after his mother's death from tuberculosis, that Jane's mother is a prostitute and his aunt Maria an alcoholic. *Une chaine dans le parc* is a subtle and touching portrait of a boy who has come to terms with the real world, all the while nourishing a parallel fantasy world.

Langevin's preoccupation in *L'Élan d'Amérique* with American economic and technological hegemony, and with the (consequent) fate of francophone Quebec, is shared by **Jacques Godbout**. The first appears in *L'Ile au dragon* (1976)/*Dragon Island*, and the second in *D'amour P.Q* (1972) and *Les Têtes à Papineau* (1981) (both still untranslated). But Langevin's serious, even tragic, tone gives way in Godbout to one that is witty and fabulous, at least on the surface.

Michel Beauparlant (well-spoken), the writer and 'monster-slayer' of *L'Ile au dragon*, confronts and eventually outwits the financier William T. Shaheen Jr, President of Pennsylvania & Texas International, who is in cahoots with the Canadian government, and tries to convert Ile Verte into a dumping-ground for atomic waste. Michel eventually blocks the scheme and dumps a bound Shaheen into the chilly St Lawrence, acting alone (within the confines of fantasy), the islanders having been bought off by the promise of prosperity. The island at the centre of the story is obviously, in microcosm, Quebec in the middle of the (North) American sea. Significantly, as Jacques Pelletier has pointed out, the main enemy is no longer the anglophone Canadian, as in *Le Couteau sur la table*, but a spokesman for American big business (as in *L'Élan d'Amérique*), who not only represents economic power but also a value system for which 'the shopping centre is the true cultural centre' that is being imposed on the entire planet. Pelletier links the radicalization of Godbout's political vision to the recession that struck Quebec at the beginning of the 1970s, with the resultant increase in the militancy of trade unions and the sharpening of their political discourse.

The remaining two Godbout novels under consideration here have other concerns. In the farcical and very funny *D'amour, P.Q.*, Thomas D'amour, a 'priggish intellectual' (Patricia Smart), far removed from everyday reality, is trying to write a novel. Its various drafts imitate in turn Biblical, exotic, and US comic-book styles and heroes before it becomes completely transformed by Mireille, the author's lover and a secretary in the French Department at the Université de Montréal, who speaks a breezy and vulgar version of *joual*. Fed up with his escapism, she dictates to him (and he types) a novel rooted in Quebec and its popular speech, claiming that the word-fund is a natural resource belonging to the masses. The October Crisis of 1970 was still fresh in people's memories when the book appeared, and Godbout, in a transposition of that event, proposes a fraternal Quebec utopia in opposition to the present 'plastic civilization'. Thomas and Mireille create their own underground group (*'La Cellule D'amour du Front de libération du Kébek'*), which sends out communiqués to the media, as did the FLQ. But these are inspired by counter-cultural poet

Raoul Duguay, to whom the book is dedicated, and quotations from whose poems form epigraphs for each of the three 'acts' and the epilogue of the novel. The one prefacing Act Two sums up this ideological thrust: 'May the voice of Kébek be a bomb of love.' The work's title relates not only to the hero, but also to his pacifist dream; while *P.Q.* in the title plays on the ambiguity between *'Province de Québec'* and *'Parti Québécois'*.

This very type of ambiguity is at the core of Godbout's *Les Têtes à Papineau*, which plays on a Quebec folk-saying (to *be* a *'tête à Papineau'*, or to *have* a head similar to that of the 1837 Patriote leader who led the struggle for independence from Britain, is to be very clever), as well as signifying the narrator(s) of the novel, the two-headed monster Charles-François Papineau. (As *D'amour, P.Q.* was written in the wake of the October Crisis, *Les Têtes à Papineau* followed on the heels of the defeat of the 1980 referendum on sovereignty-association, and is indelibly marked by it. The 'Charles' head is anglophile and rather stiff, while the 'François' head has Gallic tastes and spirit (the name is an ancient form of 'français'). Clearly the twin heads on a single body are a symbolic representation of Canada itself. The text of this short book is a journal kept for publication by Charles-François, which ends when the 'heads', exasperated by their differences, agree to undergo surgery to create a unicephalic being through the fusion of a half of the head of each. The result, however, is the creation of a unilingual English being who signs his name 'Charles F. Papineau', having evidently subsumed 'François'. In an addendum to the journal, the unicephalic Charles writes a letter *in English* to the francophone publisher in Montreal, expressing his regrets at not being able to write the last chapter of the journal (as per the contract the 'heads' signed earlier) 'in your language'. Charles expresses his readiness, however, to give the publisher some 'feedback' on the manuscript, once he has read it *in translation*. Charles's return-address is that of the computer-science centre where he now works, in *English* Bay, Vancouver.

At the end of the final 'two-headed' chapter, on the eve of the surgery, the father of the monster offers a toast to evolution, but 'the heads' draw attention to the victims of evolution—dinosaurs, brontosaurs, Armenians—and comment: 'The *têtes à Papineau* of all hemispheres, or one among them, are fated to disappear. Evolution follows the concept of "might is right". How could a frog swim in a sea of unicephalic beings?' This post-referendum work, then, cast a pessimistic look at the future of the 'French fact' in Quebec.

Among the victims of 'evolution' listed in the above are the Acadians—French-speaking people of the Maritime Provinces who are today concentrated mainly in New Brunswick, where they make up nearly forty per cent of the population. **Antonine Maillet** (b. 1929) came to prominence in the seventies as the major writer to emerge from this environment. Her novels and plays are at one and the same time a reflection of, a tribute to, and a catalyst for the Acadians' struggle to survive culturally against great odds.

Nearly twenty years ago Maillet—a native of Bouctouche, New Brunswick—stunned audiences and readers alike with her brilliant series of dramatic monologues, **La Sagouine* (1971), centred on a long-suffering but lucid and courageous Acadian washerwoman 'who was born with the century, her feet practically in water'. This one-woman show, unforgettably acted by Viola Léger, was seen by many thousands of people throughout Canada, the New England states, and the francophone countries of Europe. According to Simone LeBlanc-Rainville, the publication of *La Sagouine* (the text has sold over 100,000 copies) was 'an event of great social significance for Acadia. For the first time, perhaps, the *élites* did not speak in the name of the people, but let the most unfortunate speak for all.' Maillet's literary career was crowned in 1979 when she won France's leading literary prize, the Prix Goncourt, for *Pélagie-la-Charrette / Pélagie: The Return to a Homeland*, the first writer outside of continental France to do so. Some one million copies of this novel have been sold.

In Maillet's first publication, *Pointe-aux-coques* (1958), there is a sizeable ethnological component that is not fully integrated into the imaginary universe. But in her more mature works—*La Sagouine, Mariaagélas* (1973)/*Mariaagélas: Maria, Daughter Of Gélas*, and *Pélagie*—she succeeded in deftly combining a highly sensitive social consciousness with appropriate aesthetic forms. Her fine skills as a storyteller were already evident in 1972 in the largely fantastic *Don l'Orignal/The Tale Of Don l'Orignal*, in which she pitted stuffed-shirt mainlanders against the spontaneous, folksy inhabitants of Flea Island—a binary structure basic to much of her work—with echoes of Homer, the Bible, the *chanson de geste*, and Rabelais. Other good novels by Maillet are *Les Cordes-de-bois* (1979), the name of a windswept hillock and haven for vagabonds during the Depression, and *Crache à Pic* (1984)/*The Devil Is Loose!*, which, however, repeats some of the incidents of *Mariaagélas*.

Gilles Marcotte has said that in Maillet's major works, 'the heroes are heroines . . . . In the official, historic country—that is to say in Ottawa, Fredericton or Moncton—men rule indisputably; in Antoine Maillet's Acadia, on the other hand, they are reduced, with few exceptions, to commenting on the actions initiated by the women.' In *Mariaagélas*, the eponymous heroine is a rebellious young smuggler of the Prohibition era who constantly and totally contests everything and everyone. Descended from a family of fishermen/blacksmiths-cum-bootleggers, she turns to the latter occupation because of poverty and alienation at the hands of both local élites and distant and anonymous governments. Ostracized in her village because she struck a teacher who humiliated her younger sister, she is unable to get a traditional maid's job, and refuses to work in the lobster-canning plants because of the long hours, dank conditions, and smell of rotten fish. Besides fighting the customs officials, she and her Aunt Clara, a former cannery worker, team up against the widow Calixte, the satirized, recurring zealot, and many hilarious events punctuate their rivalry. After the unsolved murder of Ferdinand, the fisherman turned customs-officer, aunt and niece disappear, followed by many a legend. The fisherman, Basile à Pierre, holds the divisions among the poor as responsible for the death, and proposes 'uniting in the face of adversity and extricating ourselves together from misery.' The sprightly narrator is at one with her characters and uses the *nous* form to become one herself, but still 'lets doubt and mystery hang over an unexpected or inexplicable event . . . reviving her tale through verbal pirouettes' (Jean-Guy Hudon).

Pélagie goes back in time to a momentous incident in the history of the Acadians, their expulsion from Nova Scotia in 1755 and subsequent scattering throughout the southern colonies. The work is indelibly marked by the rhythm of continuity, its final inscription reading: 'Bouctouche, June 23, 1979, in this year of the 375th anniversary of the founding of Acadia' (1604). The French title, the nickname of the heroine, is associated with the *charrette*, the traditional cart given by the bride to her husband as a sign of continuity. The narrative structure—based on a lineage of chroniclers retelling the saga at a distance of 100 years (at the end of the nineteenth century, and, today, at the close of the twentieth)—is also one of perpetuation of memory and heritage. The unobtrusive primary narrator in the present relates most of the events of the epic return of the Acadians between 1770 and 1780 as they were told to her by her cousin, 'old Louis à Bélonie, known as the younger', who himself had received them from his grandfather, a storyteller of the end of the previous century, an actual descendant of the nonagenarian Bélonie who, together with the original Pélagie, actually lived the adventure of the arduous homecoming. Other rhythmic devices give cohesion and unity to the novel, and combine its form and content into a whole. One of the most important of these is the parallelism developed between the oxen-led *charrette* of Pélagie—representing life, hope, optimism—and the ghostly *charrette de la mort*, representing death, destruction, despair, and fatalism, with its six black horses constantly evoked and perceived by the wizened Bélonie as travelling alongside, and sometimes in the very ruts of, Pélagie's cart. The two *charrettes* 'compete' mercilessly throughout the narrative. Old Man Bélonie is also the source of other elements of fantasy, as he recounts legends and folk tales.

The story is structured, too, by the refrain of the traditional Acadian folksong *'Le grain de mil'*—sung on the few happy occasions that break the suffering of the exiles—and by that other refrain-expletive, *'Merde au roi d'Angleterre!'* (Shit on the king of England!), uttered when the burning of the church at Grand-Pré, or other tribulations at the hands of the British, are recalled. Yet while the tragic events of 1755 and their aftermath are often the butt of Maillet's irony and bitterness, the rancour of the past gives way to forgiveness, in the hope of starting a new life on Acadian soil after the long trek. Pélagie projects her return thus: '. . . she would forget, and she would forgive and build anew her burned-out dwelling.'

The language of *Pélagie* is largely that of the spoken word. Maillet gave it here a more stylized form than in *La Sagouine* (to which she appended a glossary), while still keeping its essential flavour and thus making her book more accessible. The texture of the language is often richly poetic, and towards the end of the novel, in the springtime of the return to Acadia in 1780, lyricism inundates the prose. But the language is also often humorous, earthy, Rabelaisian, *démesuré*, and outrageously hyperbolic. When she received the Goncourt prize, Maillet saw in it a rehabilitation of her people's speech, brought to North America from Poitou and Touraine in the seventeenth and eighteenth centuries, but often vilified as a *patois*: 'When an academy gives a prize of this stature to a work, it means that it also recognizes the status of its language.' That speech of her ancestors, in Maillet's words, has been 'distorted by the climate and sharpened by the sea, by the salty air in the larynx and the obsessive beating of the waves in the ears.'

The sequel to *Pélagie*, *Cent ans dans les bois* (1981), was a disappointment because of a contrived and unusually thin plot. Folklorization, didacticism, and ethnologism far outweigh the richly imaginative content, and one cannot help but worry with Yves Leduc that Maillet has become a victim of a situation in which 'marketing reigns supreme', and in which her publisher pushes her to produce exchangeable commodities rather than build on the solid foundations of her best works.

André Major, Jacques Poulin, and Victor-Lévy Beaulieu also came into prominence during the seventies, though all three began publishing in the preceding decade. The youngest, **André Major** (b. 1942), published two books of poetry in 1961 and 1962 and his first novel, *Le Cabochon* (The Stubborn One), in 1964. A sort of *Bildungsroman*, it is the story of Antoine, a young man from a working-class family in search of his autonomy, and has been described as 'an opening up to life and to writing'. It appeared thanks to the *Parti pris* publishing house, after a Catholic youth journal suspended its continuation in serial form. The largely self-taught author was linked to the monthly from 1963 to 1965, identifying publicly with radical, even violent, nationalism. Major severed his relations with *Parti pris* and its ideology partly because he felt estranged from his university-educated colleagues and also because, as the narrator in one of his short stories says, 'instead of saving the world, I was going to try to save myself from the world.' He then adopted a conservative-nationalist outlook, writing for *L'Action nationale* and composing an admiring study of Félix-Antoine Savard. It was at that time that Major reiterated the folkloric nationalist view of the countryside as being 'naturally homogeneous and faithful to tradition . . . where man is in immediate harmony with his surroundings', a view he had contested earlier, and would again later, as we shall soon see. Another break came after the 1970 October Crisis, when Major condemned political violence and associated himself with the Parti Québécois. He has since remained a moderate *indépendantiste*.

Major is best known for his much-praised and much commented on trilogy, *Histoires de déserteurs*: *L'Épouvantail* (1974) / *The Scarecrows of Saint-Emmanuel*, *L'Épidémie* (1975) / *Inspector Therrien. Tales of Deserters*, and *Les Rescapés* (1976) / *Man on the Run*. Most of the action is set in the fictional Laurentian village of Saint-Emmanuel-de-l'Épouvante, north of the region of an equally fictional Terrenoire. (The cycle becomes progressively a chronicle of village mores.) The name of the village is a paradoxical one in that it combines Emmanuel (the name, meaning 'God be with us', that Isaiah designated for the child whose birth would signify Judah's deliverance, later associated by St Matthew with Jesus) with *épouvante* (terror), which is also linked phonically and etymologically with the title of the first volume, signifying scarecrow. The decaying rural milieu is a projection of Major's vision of Quebec, though the tone of the book is certainly not depressing. All three novels are fast-paced; there is a good deal of suspense in the activities of Momo, the central character; the unusual coming together in a son-father relationship of Momo and the detective who had pursued him; colourful dialogue with an easy integration of popular speech; and a host of motley secondary characters.

L'Épouvantail begins like a detective novel and is centred on the murder in Montreal of Gigi, a call-girl and former lover of Maurice 'Momo' Bélanger. He has just been released from prison for theft (Gigi was indirectly responsible for his incarceration) and is now wrongly accused of Gigi's murder, which was probably the work of her pimp and his gang. Badly beaten by the latter, Momo is left for dead near Saint-Emmanuel but eventually flees into the woods with another woman, Marie-Rose. He is caught, has his shoulder broken by a bullet, and ends up again in prison with a life-sentence. Police inspector Paul-Émile Therrien is in charge of his investigation. *L'Épidémie* (The Epidemic—possibly meaning the spate of broken romantic relationships) finds Therrien, three months later, retired and living in his house in the village. Rejecting the advances of his former heart-throb Émérence, who had once rejected him and married the village hosteler, he suddenly marries her sister, the widow Julienne. His sexual activities are reduced to taking pictures of them alternately, in the nude, with the camera given him on his retirement. In the meantime Momo escapes from prison again, seeks refuge in the village, and, surprisingly, is hidden in Therrien's home, where Marie-Rose visits him secretly. At the beginning of *Les Rescapés* (The Survivors) Momo, having left Therrien, discovers his frozen body in a bear-trap the convict had set to get food. Momo and the pregnant Marie-Rose flee again to a deserted village; while in Saint-Emmanuel, Émérence's husband Jérôme is elected mayor over Dupré, the former mayor who had fled to Montreal with Émérence. This liaison, like Therrien's marriage to Julienne, will be short-lived. Jérôme is also elected to the provincial legislature. Marie-Rose leaves Momo with her child to rejoin her father, while her lover flees ever further north. (A later story by Major, 'La grande nuit blanche', is a kind of epilogue and ends with his murder.)

The critical reception of Major's trilogy was almost unanimously positive, with the author being praised for his stylistic assurance, deft handling of dialogue, overall composition, and the broad sweep of his canvas. Jacques Pelletier saw in it a reflection of

Major's nationalism. For him the three novels constitute 'a questioning of Quebec of which Saint-Emmanuel is a model in microcosm'. He based this view in part on the epigraph to *L'Épidémie*, a quotation from a sociological study of a twentieth-century Quebec village treating 'strange survivors deprived of a tradition . . . who live from anything but the soil . . . and drink in order to forget.' Pelletier was one of the first critics to relate some of Major's techniques to those of Faulkner (acknowledged by the author): the fatal marking of the characters by a traumatic incident; the shifts back and forth from past to future, with a gradual revealing of the characters' personalities; an addendum to the second volume of a list of the characters and a resumé of their traits, plus a map of the principal sites of the action. Pelletier quotes a 1975 text by Major: '. . . the writer writes in order to reveal the world and by doing this, contributes in his own way to changing it.' He sees this approach as the 'background and theoretical foundation' of the trilogy and goes on to link the writing and publishing of the cycle, from 1970 to 1976, with the Liberal regime that ruled Quebec precisely in those years—Saint-Emmanuel 'appearing like a symbol of Quebec society under Robert Bourassa . . . made up of survivors condemned to disappear pathetically.'

Victor-Lévy Beaulieu (b. 1945) is the most prolific writer in Quebec today, since the death in 1983 of Yves Thériault. In some ways his novels have parallels with André Major's trilogy. While most of the action of Beaulieu's saga of the Beauchemin family is set in the Montreal area, there are constant recollections, obsessions, and nightmares linked to the nearly mythic *petite patrie* (little homeland) of the clan, the village of Saint-Jean-de-Dieu on the Lower St Lawrence. The transplanting (or temporary displacement) of the characters from the countryside to the metropolis, with all its inherent tension and conflict, is also present. The degradation, sexual aberration, loneliness, and non-communicability of most of the players in the saga are similar to, although much more extreme than, Major's fictional universe. Beaulieu considers the *Parti pris* writers, with whom Major broke, as 'lay missionaries', and his view of ideology—as expressed by his narrator in *Blanche forcée* (1976), Job J. Jobin, who says that he believes neither 'in astrology, nor in the past, nor in psychology, nor in ideology'—is not unlike that of the author of the Saint-Emmanuel novels. There are, however, some major differences. In a number of Beaulieu's novels the line between dream and reality is blurred by the phantasms of the narrator or main character. While the tonality of Major's writing is serious, Beaulieu's is often satirical and punny (sometimes excruciatingly so), although the humour frequently masks the tragedy of broken dreams. Also, from his first work on Beaulieu represents the act of writing within his fiction, and progressively gives more and more place to his *alter ego*, the novelist and editor Abel Beauchemin.

Five of Beaulieu's novels—all from the Beauchemin cycle of eight novels—have been translated into English: *Jos Connaissant* (1970), *Les Grands-pères* (1972) / *The Grandfathers*, *Un rêve québécois* (1972) / *A Québécois Dream*, *Don Quichotte de la démanche* (1974) / *Don Quixote in Nighttown*, and *Steven le Hérault* (1985). The first novel of the cycle, *Race de monde!* (1969), introduces Pa, transplanted from his native village to 'Morial Mort' (read Montréal Nord), who looks after Mongoloid children in an institution with the same name as his birthplace; Mam, with her silent tenderness; and their twelve children, with the spotlight on Abel Beauchemin, the would-be but despairing writer; his brother Steven, 'the poet', who thinks Abel is the only one in the family 'who has a chance to resist our miserable past and our vulgar present' and paves the way for his literary career; and the eldest son, Jos, the future mystic. The extravagant use of puns shows the influence of Ducharme, and there is a somewhat gratuitous delectation of physical ugliness, putrefaction, and genitalia (the author flays the enduring Quebec taboos with a vengeance). Another untranslated Beauchemin novel, *La Nuitte de Malcolm Hudd* (read 'malcommode', awkward; 1970) contains hallucinatory soliloquies by deranged characters.

Jos Connaissant (Québécois for 'wise guy') relates the delirious ruminations of the pathetic and poignant title character who has been chased from home by Pa and works at 'Morial Mort Supermarquette'. At night he meditates before a statue of Buddha, drinks heavily, and lives for a while with a waitress whom he abuses physically (as did Hudd) following the failure of their sexual relations. (He had been traumatized when a child by having his penis bitten by a rooster.) The latter part of the novel evokes the death and funeral of the mother, Mathilde (Mam), in Saint-Jean-de-Dieu, locus of 'the tranquil world before the chaos' of the urban transfer. Jos returns home, smashes his Buddha, and decides that madness is the only way to truth. This novel is one of the most commented-on of Beaulieu's works, with psychocritical analyses predominating, and has been reprinted several times.

Sexual violence, although fantasized, is even more brutal in *Un rêve québécois* which, at the beginning and end, evokes the October Crisis, one of the two dénouements of which (the freeing of James Cross) occurred in the Montreal North of the setting. Barthélémy (Lémy) Dupuis, freshly released from a detoxication centre, returns to his shabby home after a renewed drinking bout at a tavern. In his *delirium tremens* he viciously beats to death his wife ('Jeanne d'Arc'), rapes her, then cuts her to bits with a saw before throwing her remains to the dog. His reason? She had fled their disastrous marriage with a policeman. Lémy sees his imaginary horrible gestures as 'the act of his liberation', his revenge 'against too much humiliation and shame', but realizes afterwards that it did not achieve his 'desired freedom'. It is never fully clear whether Lémy's psychotically obscene acts are imaginary or remembrances. Jacques Michon has noted a certain baroque quality in the writing, mixing vulgarity and lyricism, derision and irony.

Les Grands-pères, which was published right after *Jos Connaissant*, recounts the last day in the life of Milien, father of Mathilde and grandfather of the Beauchemin children. The plural title, and generalization of Milien into 'the Miliens' for other old-timers of Saint-Jean-de-Dieu (Milien's second wife is labelled 'Milienne II', the first is 'Milienne I') emphasizes the derisively repetitious resemblance between named and unnamed characters, all of whom are in a moribund state signifying the end of a traditional rural way of life in the barren, stump-covered locale of the story. When Milien's second wife—who, like him, regretted their marriage—

collapses, he awakens from his doze, sees blood oozing from her lips, and considering her dead hits her lightly on the shoulder before losing all control and slapping and punching her viciously. He wanders distractedly through the village, oblivious of his plan to find the doctor, and retraces in his mind vivid memories of the past, especially dead relatives (Mathilde and his first wife) and animals. After suffering a blackout, Milien is brought home by the doctor and seems to be about to join his dead second wife. His recollections are mixed with hallucinatory visions, such as one in which he kills his wife and decapitates his children, who earlier had mocked his plan to bring them back from the metropolis to their birthplace. This portrayal of sexual violence, real or imagined, directed against women (the weak victimizing the weaker), is here similar to that of *La Nuitte de Malcolm Hudd* and anticipates *Un rêve québécois*—leading Patricia Smart to see in this latter work 'the impasse of contemporary masculine writing' that brings to the fore 'everything that had been repressed in the novel of the land'.

The novels in the monumental Beauchemin cycle are divided by Jacques Pelletier into family chronicles and a second group of self-reflexive works, beginning with *Oh Miami, Miami, Miami* (1973). The two succeeding novels are centred on Abel Beauchemin's (and others') reflections on the writer's status, his creativity, his ability or inability to combine earning a living with producing literature. This new preoccupation was treated in *Don Quichotte de la démanche*—*démanche* is a play on 'de la Mancha', de/armed, and *démence* (dementia). Like most of Beaulieu's works, it contains little action and much introspection. Abel, just released from hospital, where he was treated for a nervous disorder, returns to his suburban home and reviews his personal problems (a crisis has developed in his relations with his wife, who is in Florida) and his creative pursuits, before sinking into a new depression and having to return to the hospital. He dreams of making the Beauchemin saga a new *Les Misérables*, but concludes that 'writing ... is reopening a wound, one inflicted long ago when we lived in Saint-Jean-de-Dieu.' He is obsessed by the 'atavistic aphasia of the Québécois artist and the distance that separates him from universal culture' (Cedric May). In *Steven le Hérault*, 'a parodic rewriting of Joyce's *Stephen Hero*' (Barbara Godard), there is another variant on the life/literature tension as the 'herald and hero' of the title—Steven Beauchemin—returns from France to find his family in even greater disarray than fifteen years earlier, when he left for Paris with his sister Gabriella—because of Abel's attempts to centre his writing (including a TV serial) on his family.

While Gilles Marcotte saw in *Don Quichotte* a nostalgia for a 'tribal' cohesion that was no longer there, and in which 'the individual exists only as a member of the group', Jacques Allard stressed that Abel's anguish arose from the writer's inability to find his place in the ambient society, thus resulting in his 'reduction of the latter to monsters, madmen, Saint-Jean-de-Dieu (the mental hospital). All that's left is the family, *la petite patrie*, the original birthplace, because there is no real, total country.' Jacques Pelletier, while acknowledging a link between Beaulieu's tragic vision and the referential society, sees the source of the novelist's pessimism in his 'reductive' views that Quebec has become a 'shrunken entity' in comparison with earlier times, and that history is nothing but 'murder, corruption, intimidation, violence and blood', neglecting the role of movements for progress and change.

Reflections on writing and the writer, so important in Victor-Lévy Beaulieu's fiction, is also a major and continuous preoccupation of **Jacques Poulin** (b. 1937), the most appealing novelist (with Marie-Claire Blais) to come out of Quebec City since Roger Lemelin, and one who is attracting more and more critical attention. But the subtle, muted tonality of Poulin's fiction, his (apparently) simple, classical style (short on images, adjectives, adverbs), avoidance of *joual* and naturalistic settings, and timid sexuality set him apart from Beaulieu. Yet the limpid quality of his writing disguises its complexity.

Writers of one sort or another all have an important role in Poulin's first three novels—*Mon Cheval pour un royaume* (1967), *Jimmy* (1969), and *Le Coeur de la baleine bleue* (1970), combined in a single translation as *The 'Jimmy' Trilogy* (1979)—which are all recounted in the first person. Pierre of the first and Nöel of the third belong to the 'professional' category, while the eleven-year-old narrator of the second is a fervidly imaginative 'amateur'. With *Faites des beaux rêves* (1974) (Sweet dreams!), *Les Grandes Marées* (1978)/*Spring Tides*, and *Volkswagen Blues (1984), there is a shift to third-person narration: Amadou, in the first, is a bookkeeper ('*commis* [clerk] *aux écritures*', the latter word meaning, literally, 'accounts', 'entries', 'books'), who recounts his dreams and other stories to his brother Théo, a car-race reporter, and their friend Limoilou; Teddy Bear of the second is a translator of comic-strips who lives on Ile Madame, to which an 'Author' (strongly resembling Beaulieu) eventually moves; 'Jack Waterman' in the third (a 'nom de *plume*' in a double sense, as Anne Marie Miraglia has noted) is the author of five novels, like Poulin at the time, and is about the same age.

These varied 'authors' worry about their love-life (Jimmy is concerned about that of his parents), their physical appearance, their moral strengths and weaknesses, and their writing ability. In *The 'Jimmy' Trilogy* the locale is Quebec City (especially the old section of Upper Town) and its environs, an area where the author has spent most of his life, and for which he has a deep affection. The first work is narrated by Pierre, a writer whose 'intellectual shell' prevents him from having meaningful communication with his mistress, Nathalie, and his friend, the calèche-driver Simon. Pierre takes part in an underground plot to blow up a historic monument—a symbolic way of breaking out of his shell—and is hurt by the explosion; he is interned in a psychiatric hospital. His friend Simon also loves Nathalie and sometimes shares her bed. The romantic triangle recurs in most of Poulin's works. In *Volkswagen Blues* the narrator tells his companion that while one is busy preparing a book, 'the person you love most in the world takes off with someone you've never even heard of.' This suggests another recurring motif in Poulin: the conflict between writing and living (also present, as was seen, in Victor-Lévy Beaulieu's work, and even in Jacques Godbout's hybrid neologism *vécrire*—'live-write'—in *Salut Galarneau!*).

Jimmy (a name the young narrator takes from a champion car-racer) is set in Cap Rouge in a summer cottage that sits on piles as shaky as his parents' marriage. There the youngster—thanks to a two-way radio, steering wheel, and other paraphernalia offered him by a neighbour, a ship's captain—creates his own world of wonder and adventure, marked, as is Poulin's entire fictional universe, by his SOS for affection: 'Need tenderness! Over.'

Fragments of each of Poulin's novels generate the others. Jimmy's (the author's) interest in car-racing will be a focus of *Faites des beaux rêves*, while his teddy-bear will resurface in the character of the same name in *Les Grandes Marées*; his child-companion, Mary, becomes transformed into Marie, sometime companion of the translator of *Les Grandes Marées*, or the waitress/confidant of Noel in the third of the 'Jimmy' cycle (Noel is writing a novel about Jimmy), or Marika of his latest book, *Le Vieux Chagrin* (Old Sorrow, 1989), which is named for a cat. Cats are omnipresent in Poulin's books; the same is true of the St Lawrence and its tides.

Le Coeur de la baleine bleue (The Heart of the Blue Whale) relates Noël's love affair (*'histoire de coeur'*) with Old Quebec City, but it is also in part a 'heart story' literally, for Noël undergoes a transplant, the donor of which was a sixteen-year-old girl. Left by his wife for a hockey star, Noël lives partially in a dream world in which he communes with 'Charlie, the blue whale'—as he imagines the donor, Charlotte, whose nickname is attributed to her bluish veins and peculiar heartbeat, resembling the sea-mammal's. In this work, 'a voyage to the internal pole', Poulin plays on the ideal of the androgynous being, but eventually the new heart is rejected and Noël dies.

Faites des beaux rêves is set at a campsite near the car-racing track at Mont-Tremblant. Amadou (a Provençal word for love, with 'dou' alone suggesting 'gentle'), his aggressive, hard-drinking, philandering brother Théo, and Limoilou, a young native woman he draws away from Amadou, are watching the tests for the Canadian Grand-Prix. The novel contains many allusions to themes that will become important in the later *Volkswagen Blues* (a novel of the eighties discussed below), notably Indian myths and legends, the Oregon Trail and the opening up of the American West, and Théo's fantasy of Jacques Cartier seeing the great dream of America dying: 'Every grain of sand was turned into a block of glass and concrete . . . and no one could stop them from growing, and the cages of light covered all habitable space all the way to Greenland and the Bering Sea.'

In *Les Grandes Marées* Teddy Bear is sent by his boss, a newspaper magnate, to Ile Madame, where he can translate in peace American comic strips ('Mandrake', 'Tarzan', 'Dick Tracy', 'Peanuts', etc.) while acting as a guard against poachers. Concerned about his employee's 'happiness', the boss sends a young woman, the voracious reader Marie, to keep him company. Then follow a Sorbonne professor who is a specialist in the study of comics, the boss's wife, the aforementioned Author, a specialist in material organization, a social *animateur*, and a therapist. Eventually Marie leaves the island and Teddy is forced to do likewise after having his tranquillity shattered by the invasion of the 'experts' and their 'touch and feel' exercises. While Teddy rebels against this hyper-socialization, he is at once attracted to, and repelled by, the 'Prince', the tennis machine with which he exercises and whose play is superior to any human's. Before leaving the island Teddy learns that his translations have, in fact, never been used, his solicitous boss caring only about his 'happiness': an electric brain has been doing them in two minutes per comic strip. This 'fable' (it has also been called a 'philosophical tale') is 'an ironic version of the biblical story of creation' and an attack against everything that is 'rationalized, mathematical, technological and dehumanized' (Paul Socken). But as Yves Thomas has pointed out, Teddy's and Marie's awe before the 'Prince' also shows 'a trace of the forgetting of oneself before merchandise . . . the triumph of the value of the spectacular over the useful.' Thus Teddy, like all of us, is at one and the same time a victim of these nefarious forces and his own 'executioner'.

THE EIGHTIES: 'AMÉRICANITÉ', BEST-SELLERS, AND 'AUTOBIOGRAPHY'

Numerous commentators who have attempted to discern the distinguishing characteristics of fiction writing in Quebec in the 1980s have pointed to the expansion of the spatial contours of the novel to the wide world. In this regard it would have been appropriate to deal here with some francophone novelists born outside Canada but who live and work in Quebec—like Jacques Folch-Ribas (born in Catalonia), Naim Kattan (Iraq), Monique Bosco (Austria), Danny Laferrière (Haiti), and Régine Robin (France), all but the last of whom have had some of their fiction translated. This *écriture immigrante*, as Robin has called it, counterpoises an international perspective to the narrowly ethnocentric current (discussed below). Its special character, however, requires an extended discussion that is not possible to undertake here.

Ethnocentricity has also been offset by the use made by Québécois writers of the United States, an opening-up that has been termed *américanité*, or America consciousness—not to be confused with the 'Americanization' evident in *Les Grandes Marées*—and there has been some debate about its exact meaning and its usual limitation to the US. The work most often referred to as epitomizing it is **Jacques Poulin**'s *Volkswagen Blues*.

The story begins in the Gaspé peninsula. The fortyish writer Jack Waterman, whose home is in the old quarter of Quebec City—his name was given to him by his brother Théo (we know no other)—picks up a hitchiker, Pitsémine, a young Métis woman in her early twenties (nicknamed 'Big Grasshopper' because she is lean and lanky) and her stray cat, and the three set off in his Volkswagen minibus on a transcontinental trip to San Francisco, after a brief stopover at Jack's home. The pretext for the trip is the writer's desire to find his brother, Théo, from whom he has not heard for fifteen years. (The Théo-Jack relationship is a variation on that between Vincent van Gogh and his brother. Théo van Gogh found in his dead brother's pocket a letter that read in part: 'In my work, I risk my life, and my soundness of mind is already half gone because of it', an idea with which Poulin could surely identify.) Near the end of the novel the narrator sums up their trajectory: 'They had set out from Gaspé, where Jacques Cartier discovered Canada [and where Théo was last heard from], and followed the St Lawrence and the Great Lakes, then the old Mississippi, Father of the Waters, right to St Louis, and then taken the Oregon Trail in the footsteps of the emigrants of the nineteenth century who had formed caravans and set out in search of the Lost Paradise with their oxen-drawn chariots; they covered the great plains, crossed the great divide of the waters and the Rockies, traversed rivers and the desert and still more mountains, and there they were in San Francisco.'

All along they follow clues about the passage of Théo through the same sites, eventually finding him in a pitiful state—paralysed, suffering from amnesia and institutionalized—in the coastal city. Jack offers Pitsémine his old Volkswagen and flies back home.

The novel is framed by two chapters, the first, entitled 'Jacques Cartier', and the last, 'Big Grasshopper'. In the Gaspé museum the travellers visit (and where Pitsémine's Montagnais mother cleans floors) they find the source of the message on Théo's last postcard from that town to Jack, namely a quotation in sixteenth-century script from Cartier's account of his first trip to the New World. The museum has two large maps, one showing the French holdings in the Americas in the eighteenth century, the other showing the distribution of the various Indian tribes throughout the continent before the arrival of the Europeans. Thus the framing of the novel and the two maps are complementary images of each other, delineating the two traditions, European and native, of Jack and Pitsémine. The differences crop up continually during the travellers' trip, as Pitsémine identifies with the ancient Indian heritage and history, including its most tragic episodes, while Jack is engrossed in a book called *La Pénétration du continent américain par les Canadiens français*, and recalls his childhood games in the family home near the American border, with their 'hysterical, shrieking Indians' opposed to the sharpshooters of the Wild West. The fur-trader Étienne Brûlé, considered a hero by Théo, is reviled by the Métis. There is no question that, by naming the last chapter for Pitsémine, and giving great weight in the narrative to the cruel mistreatment of the natives by the early 'explorers', including the French, and their slaughter by American generals like Sherman and Custer, one of the results of the transcontinental quest is to reshape the thinking of Jack ('Jacques') about the history of North America. We are told that writing for him 'was not a means of expression or communication, but rather a form of exploration' (a credo that clearly also applies to *Jacques* Poulin). This exploring, through writing, of the native heritage recalls the warning by False Indian in Beaulieu's *Oh Miami, Miami, Miami* that Quebec had gone astray by rejecting the Indian and Métis part of itself, an idea the novelist probably got from his idol Jacques Ferron who, in *Le Ciel de Québec / The Penniless Redeemer*, and in some of his plays and *contes*, expressed a very similar sentiment.

Pierre L'Hérault has observed in *Volkswagen Blues* 'the exploration of a culture and an identity that can no longer be seen as "pure" but now necessarily become hybrid [*métisses*], no longer hemmed in by water-tight frontiers, but rather free-moving across borders, loci of intersection and confluence.' Such a reading could certainly be applied to the passage in which Pitsémine, depressed because she is torn between her two traditions, her father's white one and her mother's native one, and doubtful that she has any meaningful identity, is told by Jack: 'I think you're something new, something that's just beginning . . . something not yet seen.' But L'Hérault is too quick to link Poulin's novel with other Quebec writings of the early eighties that put in question 'the discourse of identity'. For, besides Jack's fascination with the French fact throughout the continent, he travels with a motto that is embossed behind the sun-visor of his vehicle: a saying by Heidegger already invoked in *Faites de beaux rêves*: 'Language is the home of being'. Jack tires of hearing US singers on the radio and longs for his own, while Pitsémine sings *Un Canadien errant* (a wandering Canadien), the song of the francophone exiles of the 1837 Rebellion, and one of the many *mises en abyme* (duplications in miniature) of the novel's voyage/quest. When Jack finally catches up with Théo, the idealized older brother who has lost his memory and thus his language, the latter answers Jack's greeting (*'C'est Jack! C'est ton frère'!'*) in English: 'I don't know you.' This cultural erasure was already present in Théo's baggage when he set out for San Francisco, for he carried with him *On the Road* by Jack Kerouac, that Franco-American who had lost his (French) tongue in the American melting-pot.

Most critics commenting on *Volkswagen Blues* have stressed its reflections on the recurring writing/living conflict, and its evocation of a host of historical authors, especially American ones, like the ever-present Hemingway (a long-time model for Poulin), Salinger, Vonnegut, et al. Lawrence Ferlinghetti and Saul Bellow even appear as themselves, the latter telling the travelling couple, 'When you're looking for your brother, you're looking for everybody', thus stressing the collective (as well as individual) nature of the quest. The self-reflexive component of the novel—its preoccupation with writing—is summed up by Pitsémine's angry gesture in reaction to reading in a magazine the time-worn cliché 'A picture is worth a thousand words.' She uses scissors and scotch tape to rearrange the letters so that they now say: 'A WORD IS WORTH A THOUSAND PICTURES.'

Ralph Sarkonak and Richard Hodgson have referred to both *Volkswagen Blues* and **Jacques Godbout**'s *Une Histoire américaine* (1986) / *An American Story* as 'bilingual texts', which is surely an exaggeration, but there is frequent 'code-switching' between French and English in these works. In the latter novel Godbout's hero, and sometime narrator through his prison journal, Gregory Francoeur, is himself a hybrid, as is evident in his cross-cultural name. His mother, of Irish background (like Patricia's in *Le Couteau sur la table*), named him after her first lover. A professor and former activist in the cause of Quebec independence, Francoeur is in California on the invitation of an academic society and is pursuing research on what makes people happy there. He is wrongly accused of rape and arson because of his involvement in a clandestine movement helping Latin American refugees come to the US. His 'autobiographical' defence, written in prison, constitutes the bulk of the novel, and alternates with an impersonal third-person narration. Francoeur concludes that neither he nor his short-term Ethiopian mistress, Terounech, will ever be a part of 'the troops of the richest nation in the world'; nor do they wish to be part of that California where military laboratories are preparing 'the end of the world . . . inexorably . . . .'

This politicized, highly critical view of California as an ironic microcosm of the American Dream is not shared by other Quebec writers. Yolande Villemaire, as we saw in the previous chapter, treats rather the attraction, for some, of its counter-cultural 'underground'. Even **Gabrielle Roy** drew on the climatic and human magnetism of California in her last work of fiction *De quoi t'ennuies-tu, Éveline?* (What Do You Yearn For . . .?, 1982, rpr. 1984), a novella in which the title character takes a bus from the snowy planes of Manitoba to the Pacific sunshine. Roy's utopian vision of co-existence is seen in Éveline's brother Majorique's multi-ethnic extended family. A similar vision of California is expressed by Pitsémine in Volkswagen Blues where, at the end of her and Jack Waterman's quest, she decides to linger a bit in San Francisco, thinking that 'that city, where the races seemed to live in harmony, was a good place to try . . . to come to terms with herself.'

Experimental literary approaches, such broad historical subjects as the Amerindian and francophone tracings on the American continent, and the socio-cultural phenomenon of the American Dream are far from the concerns of two best-selling authors of the past decade, **Yves Beauchemin** (b. 1941) and Michel Tremblay.

Beauchemin's *Le Matou* (1981)/*The Alley Cat* was a great success in Quebec (more than 200,000 copies sold) and in France (more than 600,000). Its triumph has been ascribed to a combination of factors, like its blending of traits belonging to several popular sub-genres (the detective story, the novel of manners, the picaresque work, the fantastic tale, the serial), its focusing on the life of an average couple in search of happiness, and its specific naming of actual streets and well-known buildings in Montreal. The fast-paced story, replete with a myriad of dramatic incidents, describes how a mysterious, malodorous European immigrant, Egon Ratablavasky, establishes a pact with the young protagonist, Florent Boissoneau, promising him financial success under his protection. Florent is aggressive and amoral, but Beauchemin portrays him as admirable, claiming that one cannot face today's challenges (i.e. Quebec's lack of sufficient economic power) without 'dirtying one's hands'. The diabolical stranger helps Florent open a restaurant offering typical Québécois cuisine, only to plot with an accomplice to ruin his supposed protégé. He then reappears to confront the hero whenever he undertakes a new commercial endeavour. Florent is able to overcome this ruthless adversary only when he resorts to skulduggery equal to his. Wealth and family bliss follow, though the street urchin adopted by Florent and his wife, and the boy's cat, perish (owing to the malevolent plotter). One can assume that the title refers not only to that alley cat but especially to Florent, who has been described as having 'the simplicity and the one-dimensionality of a comic-strip character . . .', a 'strong and conquering personality' typical of Quebec literary heroes who emerged in the wake of the defeat of the 1980 referendum on sovereignty-association and 'the weakening of community-oriented ideologies' (Jacques Michon). But in the portrayal of Ratablavasky one can discern a more interesting sub-text. Beauchemin makes a fleeting reference to him as a Czech Jew who became a fraudulent priest and even a Nazi collaborator during the Second World War. Gloria Escomel (and others) saw in this portrait, and the general structure of the novel, 'the eternal Manicheist plot of the struggle between the virtuous forces and the evil ones'; one could also read in this work a return to the distorted vision of *les autres* in Groulx's *L'Appel de la race*. The first syllable of the villain's name, 'Rat', reproduces that of the loathed animal, and the suffix is clearly Slavic and possibly Jewish, like that of Slipskin, his associate described as an *Anglais* but whose facial features and culinary habits seem to suggest a Jewish stereotype, and who will in fact be denounced by an angry customer at his restaurant as 'a goddamn Jewish poisoner'. Following the public controversy about this aspect of the novel, the English translation dropped most of the above references and Jean Beaudin's film adaptation (1985) even had Ratablavasky speak perfect Parisian French, unlike the original literary model, who uses a heavily accented version of the language.

It seems, then, that *Le Matou*—completed by Beauchemin in October 1980, shortly after the referendum—was at least in part an act of revenge against the 'No' side, which included the great majority of Quebeckers whose first language was neither English nor French. Although one might understand the frustration, and even the anger, of the 'Yes' advocates over this phenomenon, it does not justify the stereotyped images just referred to. Political scientist Denis Monière, analysing the phenomenon of anti-Semitism in Quebec during the Duplessis period, wrote that the French-Canadian, feeling powerless politically and economically and fearing cultural disappearance, 'sought self-affirmation not by attacking the real causes of his situation, but by hitting out at other communities weaker than his own.' Anxiety about a similar perceived threat to survival was manifest in a film shown on Radio Canada in February 1989, called *Disparaître?* (Disappearance?), with worrisome chauvinistic overtones. While this phenomenon is still marginal, it is clearly present in *Le Matou*.

Michel Tremblay (b. 1942) has had a great success with his 'Plateau Mont-Royal' cycle of four novels, set in the Parc Lafontaine area where he grew up and tracing the youth and early adulthood of many of his stage characters (Pierrette Guérin, Albertine, Edouard, better known as La Duchesse de Langeais, Hosanna, et al.). Like *Le Matou*, these works combine elements of fantasy with a generally realistic approach, and are marked by strong emotion and immense empathy for the characters. The fantasy is built around the highly imaginative child Marcel, who seems to be an avatar of Tremblay himself, and his constant 'companion', the make-believe cat called Duplessis—named for a cat who was killed in the first novel. Marcel lives with three generations of relatives in a crowded apartment, and visits an empty house next door to see apparitions, four women who are like the Fates of antiquity: Florence and her three daughters, Mauve, Rose, and Violette, who are constantly knitting (for life, the newborn, as well as death) or playing the piano.

The first of the cycle, *La Grosse Femme d'à côté est enceinte* (1978) / *The Fat Woman Next Door Is Pregnant*, covers one day, May 2, 1942, and centres on seven pregnant women all of whom are neighbours and/or relatives on rue Fabre, where the author was born. They are the mothers-to-be of many of Tremblay's key stage characters—'*belles-soeurs* without bitterness' (Lise Gauvin)—and a number of their husbands are at war in Europe.

Most important are 'the fat woman', Marcel's aunt, who is older than the others but is about to give birth because she enjoys it, and Edouard, her brother-in-law and Marcel's uncle, the shoe-salesman and transvestite who later becomes known as La Duchesse de Langeais, a name borrowed from a Balzac character. But there is a large roster of secondary players too. The dialogue, in *joual*, is for the most part naturally entwined with the standard French of the third-person narration, producing an overall effect that has been praised for palpably transporting the reader back in time some thirty-five years.

The second volume, *Thérèse et Pierrette à l'école des Saints-Martyres* (1980)/*Thérèse and Pierrette and the Hanging Angel*, focuses on three little girls, the two in the title and the hare-lipped Simone (who appears as an adult in the play *Sainte Carmen de la Main*) and their experiences at a school run by nuns. The reader is implicitly invited to make a comparison between the talented Thérèse and Pierrette, and the bruised beings they will become as adults in the plays. The cast is as large as that of the first of the series, and presents fine psychological portraits of a number of the nuns, in addition to those of the three girls. Most of the action is the preparation for, and participation in, a Corpus Christi spectacle at the school in June 1942, with its hilarious and pathetic moments. Dedicated to three leading Quebec actresses who have appeared in a number of Tremblay's plays ('I've tried to imagine them as children in order to create the characters of Thérèse, Pierrette and Simone,' says Tremblay), the novel is divided into four parts named after the tempos of the four movements of Brahms' Fourth Symphony, which the author supposedly listened to while writing the book.

The last two novels of the cycle concentrate on Edouard. In *La Duchesse et le roturier* (1982) (The Duchess and the Plebeian), the action swings between the nocturnal and diurnal lives of the main character, from Montreal music-halls to the dreary store where he works. Covering the period from January to February 1947 (with two flashbacks to the previous year), the novel vividly evokes some of the major personalities of Montreal's vaudeville heyday, like Juliette Petrie, La Poune, and Germaine Giroux. At the end of the novel Edouard, thanks to a small inheritance from his mother's estate, decides to take his first trip to Paris.

The bulk of the text of *Des nouvelles d'Edouard* (1984) is made up of Edouard's 1947 transatlantic and Parisian journal, which is like a long letter addressed to his sister-in-law, the fat lady of the first novel. The two share an affection for each other, if not more, as is seen in the very moving scene of the 'Coda' when he hands the journal to her and asks for a spark of the love she has for Gabriel, her husband and his brother. The clash of cultures and 'languages', and some unhappy romantic encounters, had shortened Edouard's French odyssey, and he quickly returned to his familiar east end of Montreal. Edouard is murdered by Tooth Pick, the assasin of Carmen in Sainte Carmen de la Main, in August 1976. Hosanna, a transvestite friend of Edouard's (and the hero of the play of that name), who found the diary among the murdered man's belongings, reads through it, and we with him, twenty-nine years after it was written.

(Another novelist who has shunned the highly experimental style of the sixties and seventies to tell stories, usually circumscribed in time and place, and centred on individuals and families rather than on larger historical canvases, is **Louis Caron** (b. 1942), whose trilogy *Les Fils de la liberté* (The Sons of Liberty) combines the story of the Bellerose family with historical events like the 1837 Rebellion and the exile of Patriotes to Australia, and moves through the nineteenth century and into the twentieth all the way to the October Crisis. Except *L'Emmitoufflé* (1977)/*The Draft Dodger*, his well-crafted books—*Le Canard de bois* (1981) (The Wooden Duck), *La Corne de brume* (1982) (The Foghorn), and *Le Coup de poing* (1990) (The Thump of the Fist)—have not as yet been translated into English.)

Michel Tremblay clearly drew on his own childhood and youth for the Plateau Mont-Royal cycle. Edouard's telling his sister-in-law that 'he loves passionately' **Gabrielle Roy**'s *Bonheur d'occasion* leads me to that author's posthumous autobiographical masterpiece, *La Détresse et l'enchantement* (1984)/*Enchantment and Sorrow*, one of the outstanding texts of the eighties. Although clearly not a novel, in a period when the lines between genres have been blurred it relies not only on memory but also on the imagination as Roy weaves a skein of dialectical relationships in which past and present, ethics and aesthetics, liberty and solidarity, life and art, passion and wisdom oppose each other, yet interact.

CONCLUSION

In a recent summary of literary trends in Quebec for the French journal *Europe*, Lise Gauvin pointed out that 'never before have we seen as many short-story writers and novelists as in the last few years. Indisputably, the age of prose has begun.' She characterizes the contemporary novel as 'eclectic and assured, lively and humorous, directly plugged in to everyday reality', adding that it is 'becoming more complex, and playing on all registers of language and meaning.' In the same publication, Jean-François Chassay writes: 'In less than twenty years, the number of novels published annually has quadrupled, thus making it hard to determine a dominant current or major axis in the variety of discourses, themes and styles.' Most significant, he concludes, is that 'there now exists a progressively greater 'literary fund' which makes it possible to see that over and beyond several important names and titles that rise above the others, the Quebec novel is beginning to build solid foundations and a framework for a distinct personality.'

In another recent retrospective and prospective look at the novel, Jacques Pelletier saw feminist writing as the only trend of the past few decades to survive into the present one, in the midst of the decline of politically committed fiction (whether neo-nationalist or 'proletarian') and of the counter-cultural approach. Rare were the works being written or published that 'predicted social transformations by expressing them on the level of the imagination', and thus impinged on social reality. The most recent fiction, according to him, has distanced itself from the historical process, or expressed it rather passively. Another critic, Alain Piette, has, in fact, perceived an interesting reciprocal relationship between modernist writing and historical reality. During the seventies, when debates about

Quebec's future raged, more formalist and more subjective literary forms of writing (he calls them 'sorcerers' annals') emerged. Piette implies that writers thus sought to protect their autonomy from political contingencies. In the eighties, on the other hand, with the defeat of the Parti Québécois and the rise of neo-liberalism, the modernist trend was weakened, and more cohesive discourse and figurative representation came to the fore once again in such highly popular 'chronicles' as Arlette Cousture's *Les Filles de Caleb* (Caleb's Daughters, 1985); or Beauchemin's *Le Matou* and Tremblay's Plateau Mont-Royal series, though they deal with *la petite histoire* rather than with history on a macrocosmic scale. If we project Piette's model onto the present decade, when political debate on sovereignty is resurfacing with unprecedented intensity, then one should expect a resurgence of modernist aesthetics and a proportional drop in the chronicling of history, in either a grand or reduced scale. In fact we are more likely to see the coexistence of these two, along with other approaches to narrative in the foreseeable future. Surely in the new politically problematic climate, some writers will return to treating realistically, symbolically, or in other ways the vital issues relating to the future of Quebec society and culture.

Yet whatever developments occur in the constitutional arena in the short or longer term, both anglophone and francophone communities will need expert and truthful translations of valuable literature in order to comprehend the world view of the other, and possibly to help bring us together in a new *modus vivendi* should this prove a viable alternative. If Canada represents—as Margaret Atwood has suggested in 'Two-Headed Poems'—'a duet/with two deaf singers', then familiarizing ourselves with the francophone novel of Quebec is one way of restoring our 'hearing'. In 1976, in his Conclusion to the second edition of the *Literary History of Canada*, the late Northrop Frye wrote this apparently paradoxical statement: 'It seems to me that the decisive cultural event in English Canada during the past fifteen years has been the impact of French Canada and its new sense of identity.' Fifteen years later the vitality of Québécois fiction, which made a signal contribution to that identity, is manifest.

Appendix I

THE PROBLEMS OF TRANSLATION

The first written translations of texts, from French to English and vice versa, occurred at the very beginning of the British regime in the *Quebec Gazette*, launched in 1764. Literary translation began in the nineteenth century when successes in either language were translated into the other shortly after the original publication. The explosion of literary output in Quebec in the 1960s was followed by a veritable flood of translations. These were given further impetus by the establishment in 1972 of translation grants by the Canada Council. There has been an imbalance in literary translations, with a far greater number of French-language books being rendered into English than the reverse. In the last two decades, however, there has been considerably more literary translation into French. Our concern here, of course, is with translations from French to English. Since 1977 the *University of Toronto Quarterly* (UTQ) has provided a close and critical examination of these translations in its annual 'Letters in Canada' issue.

In a 1988 article, in which he drew on his observations as 'Translations' columnist during six years at the *UTQ*, and in other activities in the translation field, John O'Connor wrote: '. . . given the extraordinary diversity in the quality of translations published in Canada, we must never forget that our reading of them is always, in some sense, an act of blind faith—faith in the translator, the editor, often the reviewer on whom we depend to alert us to problems in the "transfusion" process.' (O'Connor and others have pointed out that in the past, unilingual English reviewers and editors were the most common 'assessors' of translations from a language they did not know. I would add that this is still a frequent occurrence today!) Furthermore some translations with serious flaws—the first translation of *Bonheur d'occasion* by Hannah Josephson and *Prochain épisode* translated by Penny Williams, to name two outstanding examples—are not only being read but are also taught in English-Canadian schools and universities as if they were authentic renderings of the originals. O'Connor has summarized the main problem-areas of French-to-English translation as the following: the rendering of colloquialisms, puns, titles, cursing; the *tu/vous* distinction in French; and the use of the target language (English) in the source text. (In Hébert's *Kamouraska and Ducharme's *L'Hiver de force / Wild to Mild* the use of English within the original French text often has an important ideological function that happily has not been overlooked by the translators.) O'Connor has also catalogued the large number of omissions and mistranslations that occur.

A perusal of the translation columns of the *UTQ* since 1977 shows the following weaknesses, in addition to those mentioned above, in the rendering of Québécois novels into English: omission of adjectives, descriptive phrases, clauses, adverbs, entire sentences, significant punctuation; overly literal translation of phrases resulting in inexact, unidiomatic or misleading diction; mistranslation of individual words and misinterpretation of sentences, resulting in actual contradictions of the original; misplaced modifiers; shifts in verb tenses that falsify the text; omission of epigraphs; excessive looseness constituting a paraphrase or adaptation; careless reliance on censored or bowdlerized versions of texts for the translation; the addition of gratuitous explanatory sentences or words; alteration of the text towards increased specificity, sometimes leading to errors of degree or fact; failure to find English equivalents for religious terms, and to capture colour, style, tone or nuances; poor choice of title, reflecting only one aspect of the original rather than its centrality. On the positive side several translators got high marks for their authentic, strong, or even excellent dialogue, fine choice of idiomatic English, sensitive capturing of the tone and pace of the original, its nuances, and minute details; clever replication of puns and apt description; and for the subtlety of their rendition of informal/formal address (*tu/vous*). Translators singled out for positive achievements were:

Alan Brown (*Orphan Street*), Sheila Fischman (*The Scarecrows of Saint-Emmanuel, The Jimmy Trilogy, Hamlet's Twin, The Fat Woman Next Door Is Pregnant*), Barbara Godard (*The Tale of Don L'Orignal, These Our Own Mothers or the Disintegrating Chapter*), John Glassco (*Fear's Folly*), David Toby Homel (*The Draft-Dodger*), Mark Czarnecki (*Inspector Therrien*), Carol Dunlop (*Deaf to the City*), and Philip Stratford (*Pélagie: The Return to a Homeland*). In the translation of *Pélagie*, we have a fine example of the rendering of the oral quality of Antonine Maillet's style: 'Alive! Captain Broussard-called-Beausoleil, master of an English four-master christened *Grand'Goule* and a full crew of survivors . . . Aye, Bélonie, survivors, survivors from midocean snatched from the furious sea...' The colloquial flavour of seaboard turns of phrase is also captured by Stratford's translation of 'laughed his salt-roughened, sea-windy laugh' for '*rit de toute sa gorge rauque de sel et de vent du large*'. Sheila Fischman, one of Canada's most accomplished translators, has also won praise for her rendering of the title of Victor-Beaulieu's *Don Quichotte de la démanche* as *Don Quixote in Nighttown*, which plays on the author's borrowings from Joyce's *Ulysses*—choosing to ignore the parodic play on Quixote's full name. On the other hand, Ray Chamberlain, the translator of Beaulieu's *Steven Le Hérault*, while praised for his use of concrete images to give a colloquial touch to the dialogues, substitutes sexual imagery for typical angry blasphemy, like many translators of *joual* and Franco-Canadian speech. Thus the expression *mon hostie de tabarnaque*—literally my consecrated tabernacle wafer (host)—becomes 'son of a whore'. Many English translations of Michel Tremblay's plays show similar distortions.

But these errors are minor compared to the disfigurement of *Bonheur d'occasion* in many details of Hannah Josephson's 1947 translation. Often cited is her changing of the French-Canadian *poudrerie* (blizzard) into a munitions-factory explosion (in standard European French *poudrerie* means 'gunpowder factory'). One could add the highly ideological transformation of Jean Lévesque's description of Florentine as '*moitié peuple, moitié chanson*' (half commoner or working-class, half song) into 'half slut, half song'! *Poudrerie* continues to elude translators, for Alan Brown's 1980 translation of Roy's classic gave it as 'powdered snow', which is closer but not precise enough. This translation elicited the criticism from John O'Connor that 'much of the colour and style of *Bonheur d'occasion* is lost'.

Penny Williams' 1967 translation of Aquin's *Prochain épisode* contains a great many deletions (of difficult expressions and historical and literary references) and mistranslations. One example of the latter early in the book will suffice. The imprisoned narrator imagines a spy for the novel he is writing and names him Hamidou Diop, a member of the Wolof ethnic group of West Africa. Williams translates '*Et si j'introduisais un agent secret Wolof ....Tout le monde sait que les Wolofs ne sont pas légion en Suisse Romande ....*' as: 'And if I were to introduce a secret agent named Wolof .... Everyone knows that there are not many Wolofs in French Switzerland ....'

Other translations of important works that have been singled out for falling short of the mark are those of Bersianik's *L'Euguélionne*, Bessette's *Le Cycle*, Poulin's *Les Grandes Marées* and *Volkswagen Blues*, and Godbout's *Une histoire américaine* —the last three for failing to distinguish the presence of many English expressions and dialogue in the originals.

A good translation, in my view, must respect the cultural differences between the language of the source text and that of the target text by the judicious inclusion in italics of key words or phrases from the original (translated), and by giving some of the flavour of the original's use of personal nouns and idiomatic or dialectal expressions. When there are switches from French to English in the original, as is often the case in Québécois texts, the irony should be indicated in italics or by another typographical device, with a prefatory note to explain the usage. John O'Connor has summed up this approach very well in defining an excellent translation as 'an authentic counterpart of the source text, providing the reader with one work in two languages, not with two fully independent works.'

Appendix II

NOVELS IN ENGLISH TRANSLATION

Listing author, English (and French) title, year of publication and publisher, and the translator's name in small capitals. An asterisk indicates a title that is the same in both English and French editions.

Angers, Félicité (Laure Conan). *Angéline de Montbrun*. University of Toronto Press, 1974. YVES BRUNELLE.

Aquin, Hubert. *Prochain épisode*. McClelland & Stewart, 1967. PENNY WILLIAMS.

_____. *Blackout (Trou de mémoire)*. Anansi, 1974. ALAN BROWN.

_____. *The Antiphonary (L'Antiphonaire)*. Anansi, 1973. ALAN BROWN.

_____. *Hamlet's Twin (Neige noire)*. McClelland & Stewart, 1979. SHEILA FISCHMAN.

Aubert de Gaspé, Philippe (père). *The Canadians of Old (Les Anciens Canadiens)*. Appleton and Company, 1890. CHARLES G.D. ROBERTS; *Canadians of Old*. L.C. Page & Co., 1905; Canadians of Old, New Canadian Library, McClelland and Stewart, 1974.

Beauchemin, Yves. *The Alley Cat (Le Matou)*. McClelland & Stewart, 1984. SHEILA FISCHMAN.

Beaulieu, Victor-Lévy. *Jos Connaissant*. Exile Editions, 1982. RAY CHAMBERLAIN.

_____. *The Grandfathers (Les Grands-pères)*. Harvest House, 1975. MARC PLOURDE.

_____. *A Québécois Dream (Un rêve québécois)*. Exile Editions, 1978. RAY CHAMBERLAIN.

_____. *Don Quixote in Nighttown (Don Quichotte de la démanche)*. Press Porcépic, 1978. SHEILA FISCHMAN.

_____. *Steven Le Hérault*. Exile Editions, 1987. RAY CHAMBERLAIN.

Bessette, Gérard. *The Brawl (La Bagarre)*. Harvest House, 1976. MARC LEBEL & RONALD SUTHERLAND.

_____. *Not for Every Eye (Le Libraire)*. Macmillan, 1962. GLEN SHORTLIFFE.

_____. *Incubation (L'Incubation)*. Macmillan, 1967. GLEN SHORTLIFFE.

_____. *The Cycle (Le Cycle)*. Exile Editions, 1987. A.D. MARTIN-SPERRY.

Blais, Marie-Claire. *Mad Shadows (La Belle Bête)*. McClelland & Stewart, 1960. MERLOYD LAWRENCE.

_____. *A Season in the Life of Emmanuel (Une saison dans la vie d'Emmanuel)*. Farrar, Strauss & Giroux, 1966. DEREK COLTMAN.

_____. *The Manuscripts of Pauline Archange (Les Manuscripts de Pauline Archange)*. Farrar, Strauss & Giroux, 1970. DEREK COLTMAN.

_____. *Deaf to the City (Le Sourd dans la ville)*. Lester & Orpen Dennys, 1981. CAROL DUNLOP.

Brossard, Nicole. *A Book (Un livre)*. Coach House, 1976. LARRY SHOULDICE.

_____. *Turn of a Pang (Sold out. Etreinte/illustration)*. Coach House, 1976. PATRICIA CLAXTON.

_____. *French Kiss: or a Pang's Progress (French kiss. Etreinte / exploration)*. Coach House, 1986. PATRICIA CLAXTON.

_____. *These Our Mothers; or The Disintegrating Chapter (L'Amèr ou le chapitre effrité)*. Coach House, 1983. BARBARA GODARD.

Bugnet, Georges. **Nipsya*. L. Carrier & Co., 1929. CONSTANCE DAVIES-WOODROW.

_____. *The Forest (La Forêt)*. Harvest House, 1976. DAVID CARPENTER.

Caron, Louis. *The Draft Dodger (L'Emmitoufflé)*. Anansi, 1980. DAVID TOBY HOMEL.

Carrier, Roch. **La Guerre, yes sir!* Anansi, 1970. SHEILA FISCHMAN

_____. *Floralie, Where Are You? (Floralie où es-tu?)*. Anansi, 1971. SHEILA FISCHMAN.

_____. *Is It the Sun, Philibert? (Il est par là le soleil)*. Anansi, 1972. SHEILA FISCHMAN.

_____. *No Country Without Grandfathers (Il n'y a pas de pays sans grand-père)*. Anansi, 1981. SHEILA FISCHMAN.

Desrosiers, Léo-Paul. *The Making of Nicolas Montour (Les Engagés du Grand-Portage)*. Harvest House, 1978. CHRISTINA ROBERTS-VAN OORDT.

Ducharme, Réjean. *The Swallower Swallowed (L'Avalée des avalés)*. Hamish Hamilton, 1968. BARBARA BRAY.

_____. *Wild to Mild (L'Hiver de force)*. Héritage, 1980. ROBERT GUY SCULLY.

Durand, Lucille (Louky Bersianik). *The Euguelionne: A Triptych Novel (L'Euguélionne: roman triptyque)*. Porcépic, 1981. GERRY DENIS, ALISON HEWITT, DONNA MURRAY, MARTHA O'BRIEN.

Elie, Robert. *Farewell My Dreams (La Fin des songes)*. Ryerson, 1954. IRENE COFFIN.

Ferron, Jacques. *Dr Cotnoir (Cotnoir)*. Harvest House, 1973. PIERRE CLOUTIER.

_____. *The Penniless Redeemer (Le Ciel de Québec)*. Exile Editions, 1985. RAY ELLENWOOD.

_____. *The Juneberry Tree (L'Amélanchier)*. Harvest House, 1975. RAYMOND Y. CHAMBERLAIN.

_____. *The Saint Elias (Le 'Saint-Élias')*. Harvest House, 1975. PIERRE CLOUTIER.

_____. *Wild Roses: A Story Followed by a Love Letter (Les Roses sauvages. Petit roman suivi d'une lettre d'amour soigneusement présentée)*. McClelland & Stewart, 1976. BETTY BEDNARSKI.

_____. *Quince Jam (Les Confitures de coings)*. Coach House, 1977. RAY ELLENWOOD.

Gérin-Lajoie, Antoine. **Jean Rivard*. McClelland & Stewart, 1977. VIDA BRUCE.

Girard, Rodolphe. **Marie Calumet*. Harvest House, 1976. IRENE CURRIE.

Godbout, Jacques. *Knife on the Table (Le Couteau sur la table)*. McClelland & Stewart, 1968. PENNY WILLIAMS.

_____. *Hail Galarneau!(Salut Galarneau!)*. Longman's, 1970. ALAN BROWN.

_____. *Dragon Island (L'Ile au dragon)*. Musson, 1979. DAVID ELLIS.

_____. *An American Story (Une histoire américaine)*. University of Minnesota Press, 1988. YVES SAINT-PIERRE.

Guèvremont, Germaine. *The Outlander (Le Survenant; Marie-Didace)*. McClelland & Stewart, 1950 (1978, New Canadian Library). ERIC SUTTON.

Harvey, Jean-Charles. *Fear's Folly (Les Demi-civilisés)*. Carleton University Press, 1982. JOHN GLASSCO.

Hébert, Anne. *The Silent Rooms. A Novel (Les Chambres de bois)*. Musson, 1974. KATHY MEZEI.

_____. **Kamouraska*. General, 1982. NORMAN SHAPIRO.

_____. *Children of the Black Sabbath (Les Enfants du sabbat)*. Musson, 1977. CAROL DUNLOP-HÉBERT.

_____. *In The Shadow of the Wind (Les Fous de Bassan)*. Stoddart, 1983. SHEILA FISCHMAN.

_____. *The First Garden (Le Premier Jardin)*. Stoddart, 1991. SHEILA FISCHMAN.

Hémon, Louis. **Maria Chapdelaine*. Macmillan, 1973. WILLIAM HUME BLAKE.

Jasmin, Claude. *Ethel and the Terrorist (Éthel et le terroriste)*. Harvest House, 1965. DAVID S. WALKER.

_____. *Mario (La Sablière)*. Oberon, 1985. DAVID LOBDELL.

Laberge, Albert. *Bitter Bread (La Scouine)*. Harvest House, 1977. CONRAD DION.

Langevin, André. *Dust Over the City (Poussière sur la ville)*. McClelland & Stewart, 1955. (1974, New Canadian Library). JOHN LATROBE and ROBERT GOTTLIEB.

_____. *Orphan Street (Une chaîne dans le parc)*. McClelland & Stewart, 1976. ALAN BROWN.

Lemelin, Roger. *The Town Below (Au pied de la pente douce)*. McClelland & Stewart, 1948 (1961, New Canadian Library). SAMUEL PUTNAM.

_____. *The Plouffe Family (Les Plouffe)*. McClelland & Stewart, 1950 (1975, New Canadian Library). MARY FINCH.

_____. *In Quest of Splendour (Pierre le magnifique)*. McClelland & Stewart, 1955. HARRY BINSSE.

_____. *The Crime of Ovide Plouffe (Le Crime d'Ovide Plouffe)*. McClelland & Stewart, 1984. ALAN BROWN.

Maheux-Forcier, Louise. *Amadou. Oberon, 1980. DAVID LOBDELL.

_____. *Isle of Joy (L'Ile joyeuse)*. Oberon, 1987. DAVID LOBDELL.

_____. *A Forest for Zoë (Une forêt pour Zoé)*. Oberon, 1986. DAVID LOBDELL.

Maillet, Antonine. *La Sagouine. Simon & Pierre, 1979. LOUIS DE CÉSPEDES.

_____. *The Tale of Don l'Orignal (Don l'Orignal)*. Clarke, Irwin, 1978. BARBARA GODARD.

_____. *Mariaagélas. Maria, Daughter of Gélas (Mariaagélas)*. Simon & Pierre, 1978. BEN-Z. SHEK.

_____. *Pélagie: The Return to a Homeland (Pélagie-la-Charrette)*. Doubleday, 1982. PHILIP STRATFORD.

_____. *The Devil Is Loose! (Crache-à-Pic)*. Lester Orpen & Dennys, 1986. PHILIP STRATFORD.

Major, André. *The Scarecrows of Saint-Emmanuel (L'Épouvantail)*. McClelland & Stewart, 1977. SHEILA FISCHMAN.

_____. *Inspector Therrien: Tales of Deserters. (L'Épidémie. Histoires de déserteurs)*. Porcépic, 1980. MARK CZARNECKI.

_____. *Man on the Run (Histoires de déserteurs 3. Les Rescapés)*. Quadrant, 1984. DAVID LOBDELL.

Marchessault, Jovette. *Like a Child of the Earth (Comme une enfant de la terre)*. Talonbooks, 1988. YVONNE KLEIN.

_____. *Mother of the Grass (La Mère des herbes)*. Talonbooks, 1989. YVONNE KLEIN.

Martin, Claire (Claire Faucher). *In An Iron Glove (Dans un gant de fer.I. La joue* *gauche); The Right Cheek (II. La Joue droite).* Harvest House, 1973, 1975. PHILIP STRATFORD.

_____. *Best Man (Doux amer).* Oberon, 1983. DAVID LOBDELL.

Poulin, Jacques. *The Jimmy Trilogy (Mon cheval pour un royaume; Jimmy; Le Coeur de la baleine bleue).* Anansi, 1979. SHEILA FISCHMAN.

_____. *Spring Tides (Les Grandes Marées).* Anansi, 1986. SHEILA FISCHMAN.

_____. **Volkswagen Blues.* McClelland & Stewart, 1988. SHEILA FISCHMAN.

Renaud, Jacques. *Broke City (Le Cassé).* Guernica, 1984. DAVID HOMEL.

Ringuet (Philippe Panneton). *Thirty Acres (Trente arpents).* McClelland & Stewart, 1940 (1960, New Canadian Library).FELIX and DOROTHEA WALTER.

Roy, Gabrielle. *The Tin Flute (Bonheur d'occasion).* McClelland & Stewart, 1947. HANNA JOSEPHSON; 1981, New Canadian Library, ALAN BROWN.

_____. *The Cashier (Alexandre Chenevert).* McClelland & Stewart, 1955 (1963, New Canadian Library). HARRY BINSSE.

_____. *The Hidden Mountain (La Montagne secrète).* McClelland & Stewart, 1962 (1975, New Canadian Library). HARRY BINSSE.

_____. *Windflower (La Rivière sans repos).* McClelland & Stewart, 1970 (1975, New Canadian Library). JOYCE MARSHALL.

_____. *Enchantment and Sorrow: The Autobiography of Gabrielle Roy (La Détresse et l'enchantement).* Lester & Orpen Dennys, 1987. PATRICIA CLAXTON.

Savard, Félix-Antoine. *Master of the River (Menaud maître-draveur).* Harvest House, 1976. RICHARD HOWARD.

Tardivel, Jules-Paul. *For My Country: An 1895 Religious and Separatist Vision of Quebec in the Mid-twentieth Century (Pour la patrie).* University of Toronto Press, 1975. SHEILA FISCHMAN.

Thériault, Yves. **Agaguk.* 1963, Ryerson, 1963. MIRIAM CHAPIN.

_____. **Ashini.* Harvest House, 1972. GWENDOLYN MOORE.

_____. **N'tsuk. A Novel.* 1972, Harvest House. GWENDOLYN MOORE.

_____. *Agoak: The Legacy of Agaguk (Agoak, l'héritage d'Agaguk).* Mc-Graw Hill-Ryerson, 1979. JOHN DAVID ALLAN.

Tremblay, Michel. *The Fat Woman Next Door Is Pregnant (La Grosse Femme d'à côté est enceinte).* Talonbooks, 1981. SHEILA FISCHMAN.

_____. *Thérèse and Pierrette and the Little Hanging Angel (Thérèse et Pierrette à l'école des Saints-Anges).* McClelland & Stewart, 1984. SHEILA FISCHMAN.

Appendix III

SELECTED CRITICISM

Containing (i) francophone critical sources consulted in the preparation of this book, (ii) the main anglophone references, listed chapter by chapter.

French-Language Books and Articles

DE GRANDPRÉ, PIERRE (ed.), *Histoire de la littérature française d'Amérique*, four volumes, 1966-1969, Montreal, Beauchemin. DIONNE, RENÉ (ed.) *Le Québécois et sa littérature*, 1984, Sherbrooke, Naaman. LEMIRE, MAURICE (ed.), *Dictionnaire des oeuvres littéraires du Québec*, five volumes, 1978-1987, covering literary production from the beginnings until 1975, Montreal, Fides. MAILHOT, LAURENT, *La Littérature québécoise*, 1974, Paris, Presses universitaires de France (*Que sais-je?*, no. 1579). TOUGAS, GÉRARD, *Histoire de la littérature canadienne-française*, third edition, 1966, Paris, Presses universitaires de France.

BEAUDOIN, RÉJEAN, *Naissance d'une littérature. Essai sur le messianisme...*, Montréal, Boréal, 1989. BELLEAU, ANDRÉ, *Le Romancier fictif...*, Québec, Presses de l'Université du Québec, 1980. KWATERKO, JOZEF, *Le Roman québécois de 1960 à 1975. Idéologie et représentation littéraire*. Montréal, Le Préambule, 1989. MARCOTTE, GILLES, *Littérature et circonstances*, Montréal, L'Hexagone, 1989, and *Le Roman à l'imparfait*, Montréal, La Presse, 1976. MICHON, JACQUES (ed.), *Structure, idéologie et réception du roman québécois de 1940 à 1960*, Sherbrooke, Département d'études françaises, Université de Sherbrooke, 1979. PELLETIER, JACQUES, *Lecture politique du roman québécois contemporain*, Montréal, Université du Québec à Montréal, Département d'études françaises, 1984. SMART, PATRICIA, *Ecrire dans la maison du père. L'émergence du féminin dans la tradition littéraire du Québec*, Montréal, Québec-Amérique, 1988.

'Regards sur la littérature québécoise des années 70', special supplement of *Le Devoir*, Saturday, 21 November 1981; 'Le roman québécois contemporain (1960-1986)', special issue of *Oeuvres et critiques*, XIV, 1 (1989); 'Littérature nouvelle du Québec', special issue of *Europe, revue littéraire mensuelle*, 68e année, no. 731 (March 1990); numerous issues of the following Quebec literary journals: *Voix et images*, *Etudes françaises*, *Etudes littéraires*.

English-Language Books and Articles
GENERAL

KANDIUK, MARY, *French-Canadian Authors: A Bibliography of Their Works and English-Language Criticism*, Metuchen, N.J., Scarecrow Press, 1990.

SHEK, BEN-Z., *Social Realism in the French-Canadian Novel*, Montreal, Harvest House, 1977.

TOYE, WILLIAM (ed.), *The Oxford Companion to Canadian Literature*, Toronto, Oxford University Press, 1983.

1. THE LONG GESTATION: 1837-1937

SHEK, BEN-Z., 'In the Beginning Was the Conquest', in Norman Penner (ed.), *Keeping Canada Together*. Toronto, Amethyst, 1978, 12-24.

_____. '*Marie Calumet* (1904) Revisited (1973): The Ups and Downs of Modernism', in *Essays on Canadian Writing*, 15 (Summer, 1979), 111-19.

_____. 'Louis Hémon's Trans-Atlantic Diary', in *Canadian Literature*, 126 (Autumn, 1990), 180-4.

_____. 'Albert Laberge' in *Dictionary of Literary Biography*, v. 68, 1988, 211-13.

_____. 'Bulwark to Battlefield: Religion in Quebec Literature' in *Journal of Canadian Studies*, XVIII (Summer, 1983), 42-57.

SMART, PATRICIA, *Writing in the Father's House. The Emergence of the Feminine in the Quebec Literary Tradition*, Toronto, University of Toronto Press, 1991: chapters 1 to 3.

2. THE MODERN NOVEL: 1938-1959

BABBY, ELLEN REISMAN, *The Play of Language and Spectacle. A Structural Reading of Selected Works by Gabrielle Roy*, Toronto, ECW Press, 1985.

LAFLÉCHE, GUY, 'Ringuet's *Trente arpents*: For Different Men But Always the Same Literature', in *Yale French Studies*, 65 (1983), special issue on 'The Language of Difference: Writing in QUÉBÉC(ois)', 155-71.

SHEK, BEN-Z., *Social Realism in the French-Canadian Novel*, Chapters 2 (Robert Charbonneau), 3 (Gabrielle Roy), 4 (Roger Lemelin), 5 (Yves Thériault), 7 (André Giroux), and 8 (Jean-Jules Richard, Pierre Gélinas).

SOCKEN, PAUL G., *Myth and Morality in 'Alexandre Chenevert' by Gabrielle Roy*, Frankfurt am Main, Peter Lang, 1987.

3. THE SIXTIES

BABBY, ELLEN REISMAN, *The Play of Language and Spectacle. A Structural Reading of Selected Works by Gabrielle Roy*, Toronto, ECW Press, 1985.

GREEN, MARY JEAN, 'Structures of Liberation: Female Experience and Autobiographical Form in Québec', in *Yale Studies*, 65 (1983), 124-38.

HAJDUKOWSKI-AHMED, MAROUSSIA, 'The Unique, Its Double, and the Multiple: The Carnivalesque Hero in the Québécois Novel', in *Yale Studies*, 65 (1983), 139-54.

HEIDENREICH, ROSMARIN, *The Postwar Novel in Canada: Narrative Patterns and Reader Response*, Waterloo, Wilfrid Laurier University Press, 1989.

PERRON, PAUL, 'On Language and Writing in Gérard Bessette's Fiction', in *Yale Studies*, 65 (1983), 227-45.

PURDY, ANTHONY, *A Certain Difficulty of Being: Essays on the Quebec Novel*, Montreal, McGill-Queen's University Press, 1990.

REID, MALCOLM, *The Shouting Signpainters*, Toronto, McClelland & Stewart, 1972.

SHEK, BEN-Z., *Social Realism in the French-Canadian Novel*, Chapters 9, 10.

_____.'Gérard Bessette', in *Dictionary of Literary Biography*, v. 53 (1986), 49-60.

4. THE EMERGENCE OF THE FEMINIST 'I'

GOULD, KAREN, *Writing in the Feminine: Feminism and Experimental Writing in Quebec*, Carbondale, Ill., Southern Illinois University Press, 1990.

SMART, PATRICIA, *Writing in the Father's House. The Emergence of the Feminine in the Quebec Literary Tradition*, Toronto, University of Toronto Press, 1991, Chapters 6 to 8.

5. THE LAST TWENTY YEARS

PATERSON, JANET, 'Anne Hébert and the Discourse of the Unreal', in *Yale French Studies*, 65 (1983), 172-86.

SHEK, BEN-Z., 'Antonine Maillet and the Prix Goncourt' in *Canadian Modern Language Review*, XXXVI, 3 (March 1980), 392-6.

_____.'Antonine Maillet, a Writer's Itinerary', in *Acadiensis, A Journal of Maritime History*, XII,2 (Spring, 1983) 171-80.

_____. 'Gérard Bessette' in *Dictionary of Literary Biography*, v. 53 (1986), 49-60.

_____. 'Yves Thériault: The Would-be Amerindian and His Imaginary Inuit', in Jorn Carlssen and Bengt Streijffert (eds.), *The Canadian North. Essays in Culture and Literature*, Lund, The Nordic Association for Canadian Studies (Text Series No.5) 1989, 119-28.

SOCKEN, PAUL G., 'Creation Myths in *Les Grandes Marées* by Jacques Poulin', in *Canadian Literature* 126 (Autumn 1990), 185-90.

_____.'The Bible and Myth in Antonine Maillet's *Pélagie-la-Charrette*', in *Studies in Canadian Literature*, XII,2 (1987), 197-8.

APPENDIX I: THE PROBLEMS OF TRANSLATION

Canadian Literature no. 117 (Summer 1988), special issue on 'Translation'.

LA BOSSIÈRE, CAMILLE (ed.), *Translation in Canadian Literature Symposium 1982*, Presses de l'Université d'Ottawa, 1983.

MEZEI, KATHY, *Bibliography of Criticism on English and French Literary Translations in Canada*, Ottawa, Presses de l'Université d'Ottawa, 1988.

SHEK, BEN-Z., 'Diglossia and Ideology: Socio-cultural Aspects of "Translation" in Quebec', in *TTR. Études sur le texte et ses transformations*, I, 1 (1er semestre 1988), 85-91.

INDEX

OF AUTHORS, THEIR NOVELS, AND CRITICS